■ SCHOLASTIC

Week-by-Week Homework for Building
Math Skills

by Mary Rose

New York   •   Toronto   •   London   •   Auckland   •   Sydney

Mexico City   •   New Delhi   •   Hong Kong   •   Buenos Aires

Teaching *Resources*

Special thanks to

Ann Hoats and Susan Maddox of
Lake Sybelia Elementary School, Maitland, Florida

Terry Cooper, Joanna Davis-Swing, and
Mela Ottaiano of Scholastic Inc.

Cover design by Lillian Kohli
Interior design by Kelli Thompson

ISBN 0-439-53134-9
Copyright © 2006 by Mary Rose
All rights reserved. Published by Scholastic Inc.
Printed in the U.S.A.

2 3 4 5 6 7 8 9 10   40   14 13 12 11 10 09 08 07 06

Contents

Introduction

In the fall of 1999 I began creating weekly homework assignments that asked students to read aloud a passage to a parent at home. Each of these lessons contained a letter to the parents followed by questions that addressed specific reading benchmarks and were written in the style of questions on state reading assessments. Each week parents signed the paper and returned it to school. This project was so popular and successful that it prompted me to finally compile many of the stories and lessons into a book called *Week-by-Week Homework for Building Reading Comprehension and Fluency* in grades 3–6, published by Scholastic. In May of 2004 two additional homework books were published, *Week-by-Week Homework for Building Reading Comprehension and Fluency: Grade 1* and *Week-by-Week Homework for Building Reading Comprehension and Fluency: Grades 2–3*.

Like the reading homework books that preceded it, *Week-by-Week Homework for Building Math Skills* in Grades 3–5 was born of necessity. The students in my elementary school are ability grouped for math, and for several years I have been teaching those students who struggle the most with mathematical concepts. Often these children are actually good at basic computation, but lack number sense and math concepts beyond addition and subtraction. They can make major errors and not realize it or arrive at outlandish answers and not notice how far off base they are. They also have very poor skills in logical thinking, measurement, graphing, and geometry. I have used each lesson included in this book successfully in my own math classes to address the areas of concern. It is my wish that your students do not have these weaknesses, but if they do, I hope that this book will be a help to you and to the families you serve.

How to Use This Book

Teachers everywhere are looking for simple ways to make their teaching lives easier while maintaining high-quality instruction. They want homework that is easily graded, yet meaningful to students and relevant to the curriculum.

Families everywhere are appreciative of homework that can be completed amid baseball practice and scout meetings, between visits to the day care center and cooking supper. They want to know that their child is making progress in math and that the homework is meaningful to their child and relevant to the local curriculum and state tests.

Children everywhere enjoy interesting, manageable homework, especially if it allows them to have the undivided attention of a parent or other caregiver.

The following series of homework assignments satisfies the needs of teachers, parents, and students. Introduce the homework routine to parents with a letter like the one on page 6. Then pick and choose activities from the book that complement your own mathematics curriculum. There is no order in which you should use these lessons, but here are some suggestions for effectively using this book of homework assignments.

Hints for Success

- Be sure to read the teaching text that goes with each lesson. There are some hints and extra sample problems to help you.

- Pass out these homework assignments on the same day each week. (Mine go home on Mondays.) Allow until the end of the week to complete the work. (Mine are due any day up to and including Friday.)

- On Fridays, go over these assignments and clarify any misconceptions the students may have had. (This step is valuable for students who are struggling in math.)

- Require that both a parent and the student sign at the bottom of the page.

- Return unsigned papers to the parent for a signature before you accept them.

- Telephone parents who are not helping students with the assignments.

- Make exceptions. (I had one parent who worked nights through the week. I chose to accept her child's homework on Mondays so that she could help him complete it over the weekend.)

> Be sure each child has completed the sample problem on the parent page before you send the paper home.

- Give full credit, partial credit, or no credit for completing the homework. (I do not "grade" them because students have had varying degrees of parental help.)

- Allow for some variation in the answers. Often parents have not done this kind of work for many years. Be generous in giving credit for completed work.

- Offer a second chance. Occasionally you will have a parent who completely misunderstands the assignment. Write a note, make a phone call, or reteach the child. Then allow the student to do the paper a second time.

- To save paper, run the parent page and the student page back to back.

> I have had excellent results from this homework routine. My students have, indeed, returned about 94% of the assignments—with a parent signature. Their mathematical competency has greatly increased and so have their state test scores in math.

Dear Families,

As our world becomes ever more complex, we realize that strong math skills may be the key to our students' success. I would like to invite you to help me help your child become a more competent mathematical problem solver. All you have to do is work with your child on this short assignment each week.

Each Monday your child will receive a math homework assignment that includes a note to you and a sample problem. Included in the note are hints and short reminders of how to work the math problems on the student page. There is also a sample problem that we will have completed in class. You will have all week to complete the assignment with your child. Please help her or him with the assignment, sign the page, and return it to school so that your child will get credit for doing the work.

That's all there is to it!

Please contact me if you have any questions concerning this project. The first lesson is attached and is due back by Friday. Thanks for all of your assistance in making your child become the very best student she or he can be.

Sincerely,

Your child's teacher

Connection to the NCTM Standards

	Number and Operations	Algebra	Geometry	Measurement	Data Analysis and Probability	Problem Solving	Reasoning and Proof	Communication	Connections	Representation
Understanding Place Value	●								●	●
Adding 10, 100, 1000 More	●						●	●	●	
Number Pairs to 100	●	●					●			
Number Combinations to 20	●	●					●			
Recognizing Patterns	●	●					●	●		
Thinking About Money	●	●					●	●		●
Number Terms	●									
Number Sense & Computation Practice	●	●					●	●	●	●
Addition Tricks	●						●			
Addition Tricks—Magic Stair Steps	●						●			
Multiplication—Magic Square	●						●			
Multiplication—The Nines	●						●	●		●
Which Operation? Part 1	●						●	●	●	●
Which Operation? Part 2	●						●	●	●	●
Decimals—Money Word Problems	●						●	●	●	●
Visualizing Equivalent Fractions	●						●	●	●	●
Terms for Three-Dimensional Shapes			●					●	●	●
Comparing Three-Dimensional Shapes			●					●	●	●
Symmetry			●				●	●	●	●
Proper Names for Geometric Shapes			●					●	●	●
Measuring Angles	●		●	●			●		●	
Using the Correct Measurement Tool				●					●	
Measuring Time: Calendar	●			●					●	
Calculating Area & Perimeter	●		●	●			●	●	●	●
Comparing Area & Perimeter, Part 1	●		●	●			●	●	●	●
Comparing Area & Perimeter, Part 2	●		●	●			●	●	●	●
Drawing Figures to Scale	●	●	●	●			●	●	●	●
In/Out Box, Part 1	●	●					●	●	●	●
In/Out Box, Part 2	●	●					●	●	●	●
Mystery Number, Part 1	●						●	●	●	●
Mystery Number, Part 2	●						●	●	●	●
Interpreting a Graph	●					●	●	●	●	●
Creating a Bar Graph	●					●	●	●	●	●
Pictographs	●					●	●	●	●	●
Mean, Median, Mode, Range	●					●	●	●	●	●

Number Sense

Perhaps the most vague of all mathematical terms is "number sense." People who have been teachers for many years still have difficulty defining it—but they know it when they don't see it! Students do not have number sense when they are confused about place value and can't line up the ones place numbers for an addition problem. They do not have number sense when they can't see patterns in math or recognize that there is a connection between multiplication and division. They do not have number sense when they have no idea which operation to perform to work a computation problem. They do not have number sense if they put the larger number on the bottom in a subtraction problem. They do not have number sense if they can't do mental math and must write out even the simplest problems involving zeros.

This chapter is dedicated to developing and enhancing number sense in our students and will help to clear away the fog for some of the most common "lack of number sense" issues.

Page 12 ● Skill: Understanding Place Value

> Be sure each child has completed the sample problem on the parent page before you send the paper home.

Teachers usually begin working on this skill in the first grade, but often even as late as fourth grade, students still have difficulty understanding place value. Try using more than two thousand of something, such as interlocking cubes. Have students help you arrange the cubes so that they can see the values of "one," "one-ten," "one-hundred," and "one-thousand." Then write numbers on the board and, working as a group, display those numbers in cubes. Change the numerals around so that students can see how the value changes, for example, from 28 to 82 or from 143 to 314. Hint: You will need to do this activity several times before students really understand it.

Answers to Sample Problems: 930 is the number with the greatest value; 39 is the number with the least value. 751 is the number with the greatest value; 157 is the number with the least value.

Page 14 ● Skill: Adding 10, 100, 1000 More

You can help students see how to add with tens, hundreds, and thousands by working several problems on the board like those on page 15. Leave the completed problems on the board and ask students to tell you what they notice. See if they can come up with a "rule" or "directions" using their own language and reasoning abilities. Often children will have a far better understanding of math if we let them formulate their own ideas and articulate the patterns and rules that they see as they see them happen. This encourages students to become active learners and thinkers and helps them stay engaged in the learning process.

Answers to Sample Problems: In 7802, the value of the 7 is 7000 or seven thousands. The 8 would change if we added 100. The new number would be 7902. The 0 would change if we added 10 to this number. The new number would be 7812.

Page 16 ● Skill: Number Pairs to 100

In most situations involving these assignments I suggest that you teach the concepts before you send the homework home with students. This assures that the homework is a review and practice of already learned skills. This activity is an exception to that advice.

After students return these completed papers to school, see if they can come up with more and more pairs that add to 100. Eventually see if you can lead them to discover that the pairs could go something like this: 1 + 99 = 100; 2 + 98 = 100; 3 + 97 = 100; and so on. Let them write all of the number pairs that add up to 100. You can do this individually, in student pairs, or on a class chart. You may want to assign a follow-up homework or class work assignment to determine all of the number pairs that add up to 50. See if they go about finding the pairs in an orderly way.

Answers to Sample Problem: Pairs of numbers that add up to 50: 1 + 49, 2 + 48, 3 + 47, and so on. Any combination is acceptable as long as each of the eight pairs adds up to 50.

Page 18 ● Skill: Number Combinations to 20

Introduce this activity to students as a "game," using the following practice problem called "Sweet 16." Copy these numbers onto a piece of chart paper or the board.

5	7	9	2	6
1	3	4	6	3
7	6	8	8	7
3	9	4	8	1

In this game, students try to add numbers that total 16 in preparation for the homework in which they try to get to 20. Remember, students can use the numbers in more than one set. Combinations can be across, down, or diagonal, as long as all of the numbers are connected. Try using many different colors of markers or chalk to indicate the combinations. It will help your students see them more easily. Students enjoy this and the practice on Sweet 16 will help them with their homework.

Answers to Practice Problem: Rings should be around these combinations:
5 + 1 + 7 + 3; 7 + 3 + 6; 2 + 6 + 8; 6 + 3 + 7; 4 + 8 + 4; 8 + 8; 7 + 9; 3 + 9 + 4; 5 + 3 + 8; 8 + 8; 7 + 9.

Answers to Sample Problem: Rings should be around these eight combinations: 3 + 2 + 9 + 1; 7 + 5 + 3; 8 + 2 + 3 + 2; 9 + 4 + 2; 7 + 8; 9 + 3 + 3; 3 + 5 + 3 + 4; 1 + 3 + 2 + 9.

Page 20 ● Skill: Recognizing Patterns

In teaching this concept, be sure to advise students to ask themselves the three questions listed in the sample problem: Are the numerals increasing or decreasing? By how much does each number change? Is this amount the same across the row?

It will be easier for both you and students if you begin by introducing patterns in which students need to see only one or two relationships in order to continue the pattern. For example, in the pattern 5, 10, 15, 20…, the numbers are increasing in value. The rate of increase is by 5. Be sure students are able to do these kinds of problems consistently before you add a third element of change—that of the varying rate of change. In the example 5, 10, 7, 12, 9, 14…, the numbers are increasing and decreasing in value, and the rate of change is not constant. Now students must find the smaller relationships between adjacent numerals. The pattern here is +5, -3, +5, -3.

Answers to Sample Problem: The numbers are decreasing in value. Each number changes by 11. The rate of change is the same across the row. The completed pattern is 97, 86, 75, 64, 53, 42, 31, 20, 9.

Page 22 ● Skill: Thinking About Money

There are two very basic concepts that children need when counting money: Our money system is based on tens, and some coins are equal to combinations of other coins. Begin your study of money by making sure students know the names and values of all of the coins. Some students may not realize that when you say the word "cents" you really mean "pennies"—that 5 cents is the same as 5 pennies.

Children also need to see how the base ten system works. The easiest way to do this is to empty a penny jar so they can count all of your pennies for you. As they count them into piles of tens, place a paper dime on each pile. When the counting is complete, you can count the piles to see how the pennies made dimes and the dimes made dollars. Each time you get to 100 pennies or 10 paper dimes, replace this pile with a toy paper dollar.

If you don't have paper reproductions of coins to use, you can demonstrate on the board how a circle with a 5, 10, or 25 in it can represent a nickel, dime, or quarter for this exercise. Continue to show how different coin combinations are equal to one another. For example, we can make 25 cents using one quarter; two dimes and one nickel; three nickels and one dime; or five nickels. Because the homework lesson asks the students to find ways to get 45 cents, be sure you do not use that amount as practice.

Answers to Sample Problem: Three dimes; two dimes and two nickels; one dime and four nickels; one quarter and one nickel. (Six nickels is also correct.)

Page 24 • Skill: Number Terms

Once again, prepare students for this kind of homework by creating a similar problem on the board or some chart paper. You may want to make just two shapes and put in some numbers to add and subtract, much like the sample problem on page 24.

There is a great value to this kind of practice. It encourages students to read carefully and to think about what they are doing before they do the computation. It is also a review of mathematical terms and plane geometric shapes.

Answers to Sample Problems: 17; 31; 5; 3.

Page 26 • Skill: Number Sense & Computation Practice

This homework combines simple practice in computation and using number sense, placing them both in a framework that students should enjoy. This is actually a dot-to-dot that children make themselves.

The main focus of this activity is to develop number sense. The goal is for students to see a relationship between adding 50 + 67, 50 + 66, 50 + 65, and so on. We want students to see these patterns and for them to use what they see to compute with ease, speed, and accuracy. You can help with this process by doing lots of these kinds of problems in the classroom. Some of our struggling learners may not even see the patterns in adding 10 + 3, 10 + 4, 10 + 5, and so on. You can develop this by having them work many of these problems (and even problems using 100 and 1000) and then allowing them to verbalize their own rule for adding when there is a zero.

Answers to Sample Problems: 22, 23, 24, 25, 26, 27. The pattern students should notice is that because you are adding with a zero, you keep the 2 in the tens place and put the one-digit addend in the ones place. Another pattern is that as the addend increases by 1, so does the sum.

Dear Families,

Although our students routinely go through the motions of addition and subtraction, they quite often have a shaky understanding of the most basic characteristic of our number system, the idea that the **value** of a number depends on the order of its placement.

When children are young, we often ask them to tell us "which is bigger, the 9 or the 6?" Taken literally, the numerals are the same size. However, what we are really is asking is which numeral has the greater value.

When numerals are listed across a row, the value of the numeral changes according to where it is placed. The **3** in the number 321 has the value of *three hundred* because it is in the hundreds place. In the number 123, the value of the **3** is just *three* because it is in the ones place.

Help your child to understand this concept as you are working the problems.

Sample Problems

We did this in class.

Rearrange the numerals in each box to create as many number combinations as possible. Then circle the number with the greatest value and write "greatest" under it. Then make a square around the number with the least value and write "least" under it.

903 _____ _____ _____ _____ _____

571 _____ _____ _____ _____ _____

Let's work on this together.

Directions: Rearrange the numerals in each box to create as many number combinations as possible. Then circle the number with the greatest value and write "greatest" under it. Then make a square around the number with the least value and write "least" under it.

1. ⬭758⬭ _____ _____ _____ _____ _____

2. ⬭483⬭ _____ _____ _____ _____ _____

3. ⬭925⬭ _____ _____ _____ _____ _____

4. ⬭162⬭ _____ _____ _____ _____ _____

5. ⬭694⬭ _____ _____ _____ _____ _____

Bonus: What do you notice when you look at the numbers of least and greatest value in each set? _____

_____

We completed this assignment together.

_____ _____
(Parent's signature)   (Child's signature)

Dear Families,

Just when we think our students understand place value, they encounter it in a different way and we realize that they still need more practice in recognizing just how this concept works.

Place value is a key component of understanding our number system. The value of a numeral depends on where it is placed—that is, the order in which the numbers are written. This homework is more practice with place value. Your child will determine the "value" of numerals as they are moved to new places, to write the value in both numerals and words, and to recognize which numeral will change in a given situation. Here are a couple of examples:

In the number 987, the value of the 8 is 80 because it is in the *tens* place, meaning that it represents 8 tens. Your child should write both things: "In 987, the value of the 8 is **80** or **eighty**."

What is 10 more than 987? In this question the only number that changes is the 8. It will become a 9 because one more *ten* was added. The numbers in the hundreds and ones place remain constant.

If your child cannot see what happens in the second set of problems on the student page, allow her or him to write the problem and add the appropriate amount each time. She or he should soon see a pattern developing and may begin to work the problems without having to write them down.

Sample Problems

We did this in class.

In 7802 the value of the 7 is _____ or _____.

What numeral would change if we added 100 to 7802? _____ What would the new number be? _____

What numeral would change if we added 10 to 7802? _____ What would the new number be? _____

Let's work on this together.

Directions: Tell the value of each underlined numeral. Be sure to write your answer in both numbers and words.

Example: In 70 the value of the 7 is __70__ or __seven tens__.

1. In 1<u>4</u> the value of the 4 is _____ or _____.

2. In 7<u>4</u>1 the value of the 4 is _____ or _____.

3. In <u>4</u>731 the value of the 4 is _____ or _____.

4. In <u>4</u>52 the value of the 4 is _____ or _____.

5. In 25,<u>4</u>75 the value of the 4 is _____ or _____.

6. In 85,7<u>4</u>3 the value of the 4 is _____ or _____.

7. In 51<u>4</u> the value of the 4 is _____ or _____.

8. In 2<u>4</u>,831 the value of the 4 is _____ or _____.

Bonus: Look at this number: 5743. What numeral would change if we added 10 to this number? _____ What would the new number be? _____ Which numerals would stay the same? _____ Why would they be the same? _____. What is one hundred more than 5743? _____ What is three hundred less than 5743? _____ What is two thousand more than 5743? _____

We completed this assignment together.

_____   _____
(Parent's signature)   (Child's signature)

Dear Families,

Being able to think in number pairs is part of having "number sense." In the upper elementary grades, students with number sense are able to see patterns in numbers, to make estimates and predictions about outcomes, and to recognize when answers are unreasonable. They know when to perform what operation, that is, they know when to add, subtract, multiply, and divide.

Another way to demonstrate number sense is recognizing the relationships that numbers have to each other. When children learn to add, we teach them the commutative property of addition: 3 + 4 is the same as 4 + 3. We teach them several ways to add numbers to get to 10. Now we expect them to know those concepts automatically so that number sense can help them solve ever more complex problems.

This homework helps develop number sense by finding pairs of numbers that add up to 100. See if you and your child can come up with a rule for finding the pairs.

Sample Problem

We did this in class.

Find eight pairs of numbers that add up to 50. List them here:

_____, _____, _____, _____,

_____, _____, _____, _____.

Let's work on this together.

Directions: Find pairs of numbers below that add up to 100. Write them in the space provided. Hint: Some numbers do **not** have a pair!

55	12	18	45	39
22	78	37	59	67
75	73	33	13	7
27	48	93	36	41
87	29	61	82	63

1. List all of the pairs here: _____, _____, _____,

_____, _____, _____, _____,

_____, _____, _____.

2. Which numbers did not have a pair? _____, _____,

_____, _____, _____.

3. Create number pairs for each number that did not have one. Remember, each

pair must add to 100. _____, _____, _____,

_____, _____.

4. Write a rule for finding number pairs that add to 100.

_____

_____

We completed this assignment together.

_____   _____
(Parent's signature)   (Child's signature)

Dear Families,

"Number sense" takes many years to develop. Adults who are "not very good at math" probably never had the opportunity to understand how numbers work and therefore didn't enjoy math classes. We would like your child to have a different experience.

The goal of this homework is to find combinations of numbers that add up to 20. Your child will probably find the most obvious answer first: 10 + 10. This is actually an important step. Once children find this one they usually then look for combinations that add up to "two tens." If your child does this, then she or he is on the road to developing number sense.

As you and your child work on this together, you may want to use two different colors of markers and take turns finding new combinations. Remember that you can use two, three, or four numbers to add to 20 and that the combinations can go horizontally, vertically, or diagonally. The numbers must, however, be in order; you cannot skip over a number to get to another one to make the total.

Sample Problem

We did this in class.

How many ways can you add the numbers on the chart below to reach 15? You may use two, three, or four numbers, as long as they are connected. Draw a ring around each set. Rings can be horizontal, vertical, or diagonal. (Hint: There are eight ways.)

3	7	8	9
2	5	2	4
9	3	3	2
1	3	2	4

Let's work on this together.

Directions: Find two, three, or four numbers in a row—horizontally, vertically, or diagonally—that add up to 20. You may use the numbers in more than one set. Draw a ring around every combination you can find on the chart.

4	7	9	8	12	3
7	9	17	3	7	9
6	11	4	6	13	8
7	5	8	3	4	7
6	13	8	11	4	5
14	2	10	10	12	8

How many combinations did you find? _____

Hint: It's more than 20!

We completed this assignment together.

_____   _____
(Parent's signature)   (Child's signature)

Dear Families,

Learning how to identify and continue a pattern is an essential part of mathematics. Working with patterns helps children discover relationships among numbers, practice addition and subtraction, learn to predict, and much more. Try to remind your child to look for number patterns in as many activities as possible throughout the day. For example, they may see patterns in the street numbers of buildings on your block, or notice that the days of the week on a calendar follow a pattern of seven.

This homework assignment asks your child to work in two steps. The first step is to identify the pattern. To do this, your child needs to see the relationship of numbers—that is, have "number sense." To guide your child toward the pattern, you can ask: Are the numbers increasing or decreasing? Is the amount constant throughout the pattern? Try not to assume that your child can automatically see these relationships. It is only after clearly seeing these things that she or he can continue the pattern across the row.

These patterns are simple to start with, but become increasingly difficult. Good luck with this assignment.

Sample Problem

We did this in class.

Look at this number pattern: 97, 86, 75, 64.

Are the numbers increasing or decreasing? _____

By how much does each number change? _____

Is this amount the same across the row? _____

Now continue the pattern yourself: 97, 86, 75, 64, _____, _____, _____, _____, _____

Directions: Look at the first few numbers in each row. You are looking for a pattern. Try to find the relationships between the numbers. Do the numbers increase or decrease in value? By how much do they change? Is this amount the same in every case? If you can figure out these things, you are ready to complete the pattern across the rows.

Let's work on this together.

1. 99, 88, 77, 66, _____, _____, _____, _____, _____

2. 2, 4, 6, 8, _____, _____, _____, _____, _____

3. 9, 18, 27, 36, _____, _____, _____, _____, _____

4. 96, 84, 72, 60, _____, _____, _____, _____, _____

5. 100, 150, 200, 250, _____, _____, _____, _____, _____

6. 3, 5, 4, 6, 5, 7, _____, _____, _____, _____, _____

7. 2, 4, 8, 16, 32, _____, _____, _____, _____, _____

8. 50, 40, 45, 35, _____, _____, _____, _____, _____

9. 3, 8, 7, 12, 11, _____, _____, _____, _____, _____

We completed this assignment together.

_____   _____

(Parent's signature)   (Child's signature)

Dear Families,

If you have a coin jar into which you drop all of your pocket change, empty it tonight! Kids love to play with money and this is their chance. As with most mathematical concepts, real-life application is the very best way to learn.

This homework asks your child to list different ways of creating 45 cents without using any pennies. Try to make as many combinations as possible, with each one totaling the required 45 cents. Encourage your child to line up in a row each set of coins totalling 45 cents. This will help your child remember which combinations she or he has already used. Instead of actual coins you can also draw circles and label each one with a 5, 10, or 25 to represent coins. Continue to help your child draw the required coins so that each set contains 45 cents.

If your child does not already have the concept of equivalent coins, help her or him to see equal amounts. For example, two dimes and a nickel add to 25 cents and are equal to a quarter.

Sample Problem

We did this in class.

Draw coins in the boxes to show ways you can make 30 cents, without using pennies.

30 cents	30 cents	30 cents	30 cents

Let's work on this together.

Directions: Draw different combinations of coins in each box to show ways you can make 45 cents, without using pennies. You can use a circle with a number in it to represent a coin. For example, ⑤ represents 5 cents.

45 cents   **45 cents**   **45 cents**   **45 cents**

45 cents   **45 cents**   **45 cents**   **45 cents**

We completed this assignment together.

_____   _____
(Parent's signature)   (Child's signature)

Dear Families,

This homework assignment will help your child not only with using number terms but also logical thinking, computation, and thinking about geometry. In every case, one of the main keys to completing this successfully is careful reading—and that's where you come in. Some students who receive this paper will have no difficulty in completing it, but many others, even if they are able to read it fluently, will still not know exactly what they are supposed to do. First, be sure your child knows the terms *circle*, *rectangle*, and *triangle*. Locate some numbers that are inside the circle, some that are inside the triangle, and some that are not located inside any shape.

Then review these terms:

digit: any numeral   **sum:** the answer to an addition problem
numeral: same as digit   **difference:** the answer to a subtraction problem

Now that you have reviewed these terms, you are ready to start. Just be prepared to assist your child in locating the proper numbers to use for the calculations. It may help your child to read the questions more than once.

Sample Problems

We did this in class.

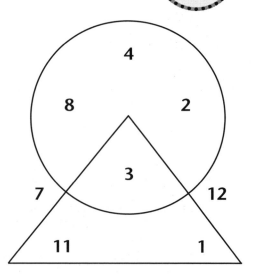

What is the sum of the numerals inside the circle? _____

What is the sum of the numerals that are not inside the circle? _____

What is the difference between the two numerals that are not inside any shape? _____

Which numeral is inside both the circle and the triangle? _____

Let's work on this together.

Directions: Follow the directions in each problem below.

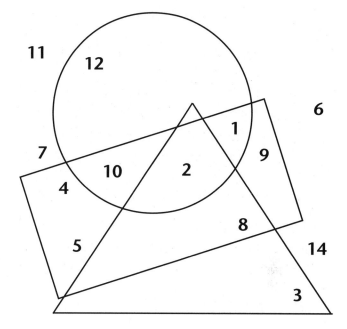

1. Trace the circle in red. What is the sum of the numbers in the circle _____?

2. Trace the triangle in blue. What is the sum of the numbers in the triangle? _____

3. Trace the rectangle in green. What is the sum of the numbers in the rectangle? _____

4. Which shape had the largest sum? _____ the smallest sum? _____

5. What is the difference between the smallest and the largest sums? _____

6. What numeral is in the triangle and the circle and the rectangle? _____

7. What is the total of all of the numerals that are not in any shape? _____

8. List the two-digit numerals. _____ What is their sum? _____

9. List the one-digit numerals. _____ What is their sum? _____

10. What is the difference between the sum of the one-digit numerals and the sum of the two-digit numerals? _____

We completed this assignment together.

_____
(Parent's signature)

_____
(Child's signature)

Dear Families,

This assignment takes five steps. Your child must first work a series of addition and subtraction problems. Then, looking only at Part 1, she or he will use the answers in order to place a dot at the corresponding number on the chart. All of these dots should then be connected. Repeat this process for Parts 2 and 3. If your child has done the activity correctly, a familiar shape will appear.

While computation practice is part of this activity, the ultimate goal is for your child to exercise "number sense." Your child may need to write out some of these problems initially in order to complete it. For example, after reading 50 + 24 = _____, she or he may need to write the problem like this ⟶

$$\begin{array}{r} 50 \\ + 24 \\ \hline \end{array}$$

It also may be necessary to write out the second problem 50 + 25 = ____ ⟶

$$\begin{array}{r} 50 \\ + 25 \\ \hline \end{array}$$

But by the time she or he gets to 50 + 26 = _____, hopefully your child will see a pattern and know the answer without computing it. Children should recognize that as the addend becomes 1 larger each time, so should the sum. If your child does not make this connection, allow her or him to continue writing and solving the problems as in the examples above. Encourage writing the problems side by side on the paper so that when the activity is complete you can ask whether she or he notices any pattern and/or can explain the pattern that is there. Having children verbalize the pattern will strengthen their number sense even more.

Sample Problems

We did this in class.

Work these problems. Then look for a pattern that makes working them easier.

$$\begin{array}{r} 20 \\ + 2 \\ \hline \end{array} \qquad \begin{array}{r} 20 \\ + 3 \\ \hline \end{array} \qquad \begin{array}{r} 20 \\ + 4 \\ \hline \end{array} \qquad \begin{array}{r} 20 \\ + 5 \\ \hline \end{array} \qquad \begin{array}{r} 20 \\ + 6 \\ \hline \end{array} \qquad \begin{array}{r} 20 \\ + 7 \\ \hline \end{array}$$

Explain how it makes these problems easy to work.

_____

_____

Skill: **Number Sense & Computation Practice**

Let's work on this together.

Directions: Complete the addition and subtraction problems. Then locate the answers to each problem on the chart. Connect the dots in order for Part 1, then Part 2, and finally, Part 3.

Part 1

50 + 24 = __74__
50 + 25 = _____
50 + 26 = _____
50 + 27 = _____
50 + 38 = _____
50 + 48 = _____
50 + 58 = _____
50 + 67 = _____
50 + 66 = _____
50 + 65 = _____
50 + 64 = _____
50 + 53 = _____
50 + 43 = _____
50 + 33 = _____
50 + 24 = _____

1	2	3	4	5	6	7	8	9	10
11	12	13	14	15	16	17	18	19	20
21	22	23	24	25	26	27	28	29	30
31	32	33	34	35	36	37	38	39	40
41	42	43	44	45	46	47	48	49	50
51	52	53	54	55	56	57	58	59	60
61	62	63	64	65	66	67	68	69	70
71	72	73	74	75	76	77	78	79	80
81	82	83	84	85	86	87	88	89	90
91	92	93	94	95	96	97	98	99	100
101	102	103	104	105	106	107	108	109	110
111	112	113	114	115	116	117	118	119	120
121	122	123	124	125	126	127	128	129	130

Part 2

100 − 52 = _____
100 − 53 = _____
100 − 54 = _____
100 − 55 = _____
100 − 56 = _____
100 − 57 = _____
100 − 67 = _____
100 − 66 = _____
100 − 76 = _____
100 − 86 = _____
100 − 85 = _____
100 − 84 = _____
100 − 83 = _____
100 − 73 = _____
100 − 63 = _____
100 − 62 = _____
100 − 52 = _____

Part 3

50 − 6 = _____   50 + 26 = _____
50 + 4 = _____   50 + 27 = _____
50 + 14 = _____   50 + 17 = _____
50 + 24 = _____   50 + 7 = _____
50 + 25 = _____   50 − 3 = _____

We completed this assignment together.

_____   _____
(Parent's signature)   (Child's signature)

Computation

By the time students reach third, fourth, or fifth grade, we assume that they should have a certain confidence and consistency with basic computation skills. Often, however, we still see students counting on their fingers, trying to subtract "upside down" (subtracting the top number from the bottom one), and generally struggling because they seem to think that every arithmetic problem is new and unique for the situation.

The activities in this section are intended to help students improve their computation skills by teaching them some handy tricks and by helping them to see number patterns. Be sure to remind students of these lessons each time you present computation strategies. Students will need to do each operation several times and have lots of practice before real competency will be present.

Page 32 ◦ Skill: Addition Tricks

Because addition and subtraction can seem so easy to adults, it is possible to become frustrated with students' lack of skill in these areas, especially if we see children counting on their fingers when they are in the third and fourth grades. These activities provide alternatives to that most basic form of problem solving.

> Be sure each child has completed the sample problem on the parent page before you send the paper home.

Do not insist that students master addition and subtraction before you move on to other mathematics skills. You will probably have to teach these skills, including doubles and doubles plus one, all year long. Consider having one day of the week become a day for skills review and practice. On this day go over all kinds of math vocabulary and practice basic facts with computer games, flash cards, and paper. In the meantime, continue to cover graphing, geometry, measurement, and so on. Come back to addition and subtraction occasionally.

Answers to Sample Problems: 6, 10, 14; 7, 11, 15; 8, 13, 11; 10, 10, 10, 10, 10.

Page 34 ◦ Skill: Addition Tricks—Magic Stair Steps

While most of the activities in this book can be done in almost any order, this particular page should be done only after completing previous lessons on doubles, doubles plus one, counting up, and finding tens. Here are some suggestions for other uses of this activity:

● Have students complete this as a timed test.

● Try using this page as a review.

● Copy this page for classroom use and complete this several times during the school year.

● Make a chart like the one in the activity to hang in the classroom. Allow students to use various colored markers to make rings around the number patterns. They will enjoy seeing which numbers appear most and least often.

- Make a big deal out of memorizing the Magic Stair Steps problems. If students can just learn these, the rest of addition is fairly easy.

Answers to Sample Problem:

+	1	2	3
1	2	3	4
2	3	4	5
3	4	5	6

Page 36 ● Skill: Multiplication Facts—Magic Square

Teaching my students about the Magic Square is one of the best things I have ever done for them. First they must realize that they can complete most of the multiplication chart (remind them that there are 100 facts here!) with the easiest answers such as 1 x 1 and 2 x 2. Then when they see that 3 x 4 is the same as 4 x 3, the chart gets even easier. Students realize that although learning multiplication facts can be difficult, there are essentially only six problems they need to memorize. All of the rest can be figured out fairly easily.

Answers to Sample Problem:

x	1	2	3
1	1	2	3
2	2	4	6
3	3	6	9

Page 38 ● Skill: Multiplication Facts—The Nines

Kids love to learn the nines times table because it has such an interesting pattern.

To teach this trick, place an adhesive dot on the left pinkie finger of each child in the classroom, and on your own. Next draw a vertical line on the chalkboard and step to the side of it. With your back to the classroom, hold your hands on the chalkboard and spread out all of your fingers with the left pinkie finger to the right of the line. Ask your class to hold their hands out in front of them. Tell them that the finger with the mark is finger number 1 and proceed to number the rest of the fingers (including the thumbs) until you get to 10.

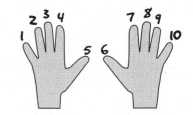

Then try some finger multiplication. Begin with 9 times 4. Start at finger number 1 (the pinkie) and count to finger number 4. Fold down finger number 4 (the index finger). Move your hands so that the folded down finger is on the line you drew on the chalkboard. The number of fingers remaining on the left side of the line tells how many tens are in the answer; the number of fingers remaining on the right side of the line tells how many ones are in the answer, thus the answer is 36.

For those still struggling to understand, have them use a piece of paper divided by a vertical line and the words "tens" and "ones" on either side at the top of the page. Help the child move her or his hands across the line as necessary to see the answers.

Answers to Sample Problem:

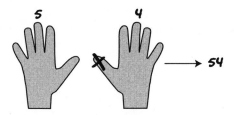

Page 40 ● Skill: Which Operation? Part I

One of the most important concepts math students need is knowing the different operations to perform and when to perform them. You can help with this by making sure students are aware that two operations will create an answer that is a larger number than any of those with which they began (addition and multiplication) and two operations will create an answer that is a smaller number than the largest one with which they began (subtraction and division).

Help students master this simple concept by pausing after each word problem and asking students to decide if the answer at the end of the question should be larger or smaller than any of the numbers they currently have. Then, after they have completed their computation, have them revisit this question and determine whether the number is appropriate to the question.

To act as a prompt, try creating a chart that is headed with "Addition/Multiplication" and "Subtraction/ Division." During the school year, if you come across clue words when the class is doing word problems, add those clues to the proper side of the chart. When you are finished, you will probably have listed under "Addition/Multiplication" terms such as *in all*, *total*, and *all together*. Under "Subtraction/ Division," you should have terms such as *how much more than, larger than, smaller than,* and *less than*. Remind students to look at this chart all year long and to continue to ask themselves what operation to perform and if the resulting number should be larger or smaller than those with which they began.

Answers to Sample Problems: clue: together, 119; clue: how many more, 33.

Page 42 • Skill: Which Operation? Part 2

While knowing which operation to perform in a word problem is a key skill, it is often one of the most difficult for students to grasp. Providing plenty of practice is an essential step.

This homework activity requires reading the problems very carefully because they include more than one step. Review the clue words with students so they will be looking out for these terms.

Answers to Sample Problems: clue: divides evenly, multiplication or addition, division, 10 pieces; clue: divide evenly, subtraction, division, 200 blocks.

Page 44 • Skill: Decimals—Money Word Problems

This homework assignment contains money word problems that use simple addition and subtraction. However, students can still have a lot of difficulty with this concept when they are working independently.

To solve these word problems students will need to do two things. First, they must remember to line up decimals correctly. Then they must use mathematical information in both textual and numerical form. Students need lots of practice with both of these skills. Have students work in teams of two, three, or four to create some problems of their own that are similar to those on page 45. Then ask students to pass the problems to a different team to solve.

Answers to Sample Problem: $9.82.

Page 46 • Skill: Visualizing Equivalent Fractions

We often encourage students to draw figures to help them solve problems involving fractions. Frequently, we demonstrate the pizza analogy by drawing circles and dividing them accordingly. While students may be able to interpret pre-existing circles divided into fractions, it is very difficult for students to draw these themselves. Because it is much easier to accurately split a rectangle than a circle, have students use rectangles when they need to split a shape into fractional parts.

This homework activity will help students to visualize equivalent fractions. After students have completed the homework, write the following equivalent fractions on the board: $\frac{1}{2}$, $\frac{2}{4}$, ___, $\frac{4}{8}$, ___, ___, $\frac{7}{14}$, $\frac{8}{16}$, ___, ___. Point out from their homework that $\frac{1}{2}$ is exactly the same size as $\frac{2}{4}$ and $\frac{4}{8}$ and $\frac{8}{16}$. Ask for a volunteer to describe why $\frac{7}{14}$ would be equivalent to $\frac{1}{2}$. See if students can find a pattern and fill in the missing numbers. Challenge the class to continue the pattern past what you have written.

Answers to Sample Problem: 1 bar shaded, 3 bars shaded, 6 bars shaded; $\frac{1}{6}$; $\frac{6}{6}$; $\frac{3}{6}$.

Dear Families,

Adding numerals is one of the first math skills students learn. Yet addition remains difficult for many students. You can help your child become faster and more accurate with addition problems by teaching her or him four simple addition tricks:

1. The easiest trick to memorize is "doubles." Use pennies to illustrate 1 + 1, 2 + 2, 3 + 3, and so on, up to 12 + 12.

2. Another easy trick is "doubles plus one." When your child encounters 5 + 6, she or he can simply think 5 + 5 = 10, so 5 + 6 is 1 more: 11.

3. The third addition trick is to count up from the larger addend. For example, in the problem 3 + 6, the fastest way to get the answer is to start at 6 and count up 3 more. Many students will start at the 3 and count up 6 because the 3 came first in the problem. That approach also works.

4. The fourth trick is to recognize the many ways to make 10. Students can learn to add long columns of figures by noticing 1 + 9, 2 + 8, 3 + 7, 4 + 6, 5 + 5.

$$12 + 7 + 8 + 3 =$$
$$10 + 10 + 10 = 30$$

Sample Problems

We did this in class.

Write the answers to these doubles problems:

3 + 3 = _____   5 + 5 = _____   7 + 7 = _____

Write the answers to these "doubles plus one" problems:

3 + 4 = _____   5 + 6 = _____   7 + 8 = _____

Write the answers to these "count up" problems:

3 + 5 = _____   5 + 8 = _____   7 + 4 = _____

Write the answers to these "finding tens" problems:

1 + 9 = _____   2 + 8 = _____   3 + 7 = _____   4 + 6 = _____   5 + 5 = _____

Directions: Look closely at every addition problem. Before you begin working, use a red crayon or marker to trace boxes that contain a "doubles" problem. Use blue to trace boxes that contain "doubles plus one" problems. Use green to trace boxes in which two numbers in the ones place add up to 10.

1.
$$\begin{array}{r} 4 \\ + 4 \\ \hline \end{array}$$

2.
$$\begin{array}{r} 6 \\ + 6 \\ \hline \end{array}$$

3.
$$\begin{array}{r} 8 \\ + 8 \\ \hline \end{array}$$

4.
$$\begin{array}{r} 9 \\ + 9 \\ \hline \end{array}$$

5.
$$\begin{array}{r} 7 \\ + 7 \\ \hline \end{array}$$

6.
$$\begin{array}{r} 11 \\ + 11 \\ \hline \end{array}$$

7.
$$\begin{array}{r} 12 \\ + 12 \\ \hline \end{array}$$

8.
$$\begin{array}{r} 10 \\ + 10 \\ \hline \end{array}$$

9.
$$\begin{array}{r} 6 \\ + 7 \\ \hline \end{array}$$

10.
$$\begin{array}{r} 10 \\ + 11 \\ \hline \end{array}$$

11.
$$\begin{array}{r} 5 \\ + 5 \\ \hline \end{array}$$

12.
$$\begin{array}{r} 55 \\ + 75 \\ \hline \end{array}$$

13.
$$\begin{array}{r} 9 \\ + 10 \\ \hline \end{array}$$

14.
$$\begin{array}{r} 7 \\ + 8 \\ \hline \end{array}$$

15.
$$\begin{array}{r} 11 \\ + 12 \\ \hline \end{array}$$

16.
$$\begin{array}{r} 12 \\ + 38 \\ \hline \end{array}$$

17.
$$\begin{array}{r} 41 \\ + 29 \\ \hline \end{array}$$

18.
$$\begin{array}{r} 64 \\ + 46 \\ \hline \end{array}$$

We completed this assignment together.

_____
(Parent's signature)

_____
(Child's signature)

Dear Families,

To complete the chart on the student page, your child will write the sums for each pair of numbers—one from the top of the grid and one from the side. Following the example in the chart (see the next page), if you start at the 5 on the top row and the 4 in the side column and move one finger down from the 5 and the other across from the 4, the place where these two fingers meet is where 9 should go.

Your child will probably need lots of help from you to get the hang of completing numbers on a grid, but this exercise is worth it and it actually goes very quickly once she or he sees the patterns emerging.

You will notice that some boxes are shaded. These are the Magic Stair Steps and are typically the most difficult addition problems for children. Help your child memorize these few problems in the Magic Stair Steps and addition should get much easier for her or him.

Sample Problem

We did this in class.

Write the sum of the numbers as you go across and down the chart.

+	1	2	3
1			
2		4	
3			

Let's work on this together.

Directions: In each of the boxes, write the answer to an addition problem. Simply choose a number from the top row and move down the column under it until you are across from a number in the column going down the side. Add these two numbers and write the answer in the box. For example, put your finger on the number 5 in the top row. Now move down that row until you are level with the 4 in the column at the side. Since 5 + 4 = 9, a 9 goes in that box.

+	1	2	3	4	5	6	7	8	9	10
1										
2										
3										
4					9					
5										
6										
7										
8										
9										
10										

We completed this assignment together.

_____
(Parent's signature)

_____
(Child's signature)

Dear Families,

Quick! What is 7 x 8? Did you have to stop and think for a moment before you answered? Have you ever noticed that some multiplication facts are almost automatic, yet others have been giving you difficulty for years? This homework will help your child with the most difficult multiplication facts. You will still need to practice memorizing facts with your child, but after she or he learns the Magic Square problems, multiplication will get a lot easier.

There are already several answers completed on the multiplication chart (see the next page). Following one example, if you start at the 2 in the top row and the 2 in the side column, and move one finger down and the other across the row until they meet, this is where the answer is written (2 x 2 = 4). Continue this process on the page until every block is filled in.

You will notice that some boxes are shaded. These are the Magic Square multiplication problems. While all of the other multiplication problems are fairly easy to get, these are the ones that actually are the most difficult. Your child will need to memorize these problems. Hint: There are really only six to memorize because 6 x 7 and 7 x 6 have the same answer and 7 x 8 and 8 x 7 have the same answer.

Sample Problem

We did this in class.

Write the product of the numbers as you go across and down the chart.

X	1	2	3
1			
2		4	
3			

Let's work on this together.

Directions: Think about the multiplication facts that you already know. Which ones are the easiest for you? The ones? The fives? Look at the chart below. Complete the chart for the easy facts first. We filled in some answers for you.

X	1	2	3	4	5	6	7	8	9	10
1										
2		4								
3										
4					20					40
5										
6										
7	7									
8										
9					45					
10										

The nine shaded boxes may be the most difficult to complete. Here are the answers to these problems:

6 x 6 = 36	6 x 7 = 42	6 x 8 = 48
7 x 6 = 42	7 x 7 = 49	7 x 8 = 56
8 x 6 = 48	8 x 7 = 56	8 x 8 = 64

These are called the Magic Square problems. They are the ones you have to memorize.

We completed this assignment together.

_____

(Parent's signature)

_____

(Child's signature)

Dear Families,

Learning the nines multiplication facts can seem difficult. The following three tricks should make it easier:

1. In every answer to a nines problem, the digits will add up to 9. Notice 2 x 9 = 18. In the answer, 18, 1 + 8 = 9. The same is true of 7 x 9 = 63. The 6 and 3 also add to 9.

2. The answers to the nines times table have numerals in descending order in the ones place and ascending order in the tens place. Look at this list of answers: 9, 18, 27, 36, 45, 54, and so on. See how the numbers in the ones place get smaller while those in the tens place increase in value?

3. Use your hands! Spread your fingers apart and look at your hands. Give each finger and thumb a number, starting with the pinky finger on your left hand (number 1) and moving across to the pinky finger on your right hand (number 10). 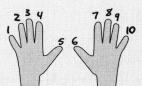 When you are doing the nines times table, you can get the answer to each problem by using your fingers. For example, to solve 9 x 3, you will need to use the finger that you designated as finger number 3. Fold that finger down and look at your fingers again. The numbers of fingers on the left of the folded finger tell how many tens are in the answer and the number of fingers on the right of the folded finger tell how many ones are in the answer. If you are looking at your hands with finger number 3 folded down, you should have two fingers to the left of the folded finger and seven fingers to the right of the folded finger. This means that the answer to 9 x 3 is 27. Try it with other numbers!

Sample Problem

○ ○

We did this in class.

How much is 9 x 6? Show this with your hands!
On the picture, cross out the finger you folded down.

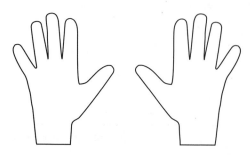

Let's work on this together.

Directions: Start by completing the chart of the nines times table at right. Then answer the questions below.

1. Look at the numerals in just the ones places in the answers. Notice what they do if you read from top to bottom. What do you see?

_____

Now look at the numerals in the tens places. What do you see?

_____

2. Review the answers in the nines chart. What would you get if you added the digits in the answer together? For example, in the problem 9 x 2 = 18, what do you get if you add 1 + 8? You get 9. What would you get if you added the digits in the other answers together? _____ What can you say about all of the answers to nines problems?

_____

9 x 1 = _____

9 x 2 = _____

9 x 3 = _____

9 x 4 = _____

9 x 5 = _____

9 x 6 = _____

9 x 7 = _____

9 x 8 = _____

9 x 9 = _____

9 x 10 = _____

3. Look again at the nines chart. This time compare the bottom answer and the top one. Do you notice that they are 9 and 90? What do you notice if you look at the next answer up from 90 and the next answer down from 9? Do you see 81 and 18? What happens to these answers as you go up and down the column?

_____

Does it work for all of the answers? _____

We completed this assignment together.

_____   _____
(Parent's signature)   (Child's signature)

Dear Families,

One of the biggest difficulties students have with word problems is not in the actual computation itself, but knowing which operation to perform at which time. Often students produce outlandish answers to problems and never realize how far off base they actually are. This lesson was designed to help clear up some of this confusion.

Our math class has been stressing two basic computation concepts. First, two operations (addition and multiplication) will produce a number larger than the ones with which we began, and two other operations (subtraction and division) produce a number that is smaller than the largest one with which we began.

The second concept is that most word problems contain some clue words that tell us if the answer should be larger or smaller than the numbers with which we began. In this homework your child will look for and underline those clue words.

Sample Problems

We did this in class.

Anna and Zoran are both collecting marbles. Anna has 51 marbles

and Zoran has 68. How many marbles do they have together?

Mark the clue word before you answer the question.

Will your answer be larger or smaller than the numbers in the story? _____

Write your answer here: _____

Abby and Frank are also collecting marbles. Frank has 86 and Abby has 53.

How many more marbles does Frank have than Abby?

Mark the clue words before you answer the question.

Will your answer be larger or smaller than the numbers in the story? _____

Write your answer here: _____

Let's work on this together.

Directions: As you work the word problems below try something special. Look for the clue words that tell you whether to add, subtract, multiply, or divide. (These are called operations.) Use a crayon or marker to circle or highlight any clue words that tell you what operation to perform. Be sure to show your work.

1. William has 346 baseball cards. Robert has 295.

How many baseball cards do they have together?

Mark the clue word.

Will your answer be larger or smaller than the numbers

listed in the story? _____

Write your answer here: _____

2. Savannah went to the mall with $17.50. She spent $9.25

on new jewelry. How much money did she have left?

Mark the clue word.

Will your answer be larger or smaller than the numbers

listed in the story? _____

Write your answer here: _____

3. Jameelah and Victoria like to jump rope. Jameelah jumped

78 times without missing. Victoria could only jump 43 times.

How many more times did Jameelah jump than Victoria?

Mark the clue words.

Will your answer be larger or smaller than the numbers

listed in the story? _____

Write your answer here: _____

We completed this assignment together.

_____   _____
(Parent's signature)   (Child's signature)

Dear Families,

The more practice students have with solving word problems, the less challenging the problems become. As we explored in Which Operation? Part 1, one of the biggest difficulties students have with computation problems is not in the actual computation itself, but knowing which operation to perform at which time. It is important for students to look for clue words that indicate if the answer to the problem should be larger or smaller than the numbers with which we began.

In this homework your child will look for and underline those clue words. However, she or he should also take extra care reading these problems because they feature more than one operation. Arriving at the correct answer will require more than one step.

As a reminder, two operations (addition and multiplication) produce a number larger than the ones with which we began and two other operations (subtraction and division) produce a number that is smaller than the largest one with which we began.

Sample Problems

We did this in class.

Julia brought 2 bags of candy to school, each containing 20 pieces.

She wants share it with her friends Taylor, Rachel, and Hannah.

How many pieces will each girl get if she divides all of the candy evenly?

Mark the clue words.

Which operation will you do first? _____

Which operation will you do next? _____

Write your answer here: _____

Xavier, Warren, and Norma love to play with interlocking blocks. Warren has 602 pieces. Since 2 pieces are cracked, he sets them aside. How can he divide the rest of them evenly for himself and his friends?

Mark the clue words.

Which operation will you do first? _____

Which operation will you do next? _____

Write your answer here: _____

Let's work on this together.

Directions: As you work the word problems below try something special. Look for the clue words that tell you whether to add, subtract, multiply, or divide. (These are called operations.) Use a crayon or marker to circle or highlight the clue words that tell you what operations to perform. Be sure to show your work.

1. Kira is helping her teacher set up a science project. There are 21 students in class, who are divided into groups of 3. She needs to pass out 6 sticks to each group. How many sticks does she need altogether?

Mark your clue words.

Which operation will you do first? _____

Which operation will you do next? _____

Write your answer here: _____

2. Ben and his brother Nathan went to the food court at the mall. Ben spent $1.99 for a burger and 99 cents for a side order of french fries. Nathan spent two dollars on a slice of pizza and seventy-five cents on a drink. Who spent more? By how much?

Mark your clue words.

Which operation will you do first? _____

Which operation will you do next? _____

Write your answer here: _____

3. After school during January, Jamal read 1 biography, 2 mysteries, and 2 science fiction books. If it took him 5 days to read each book, how many days did he read altogether?

Mark your clue words.

Which operation will you do first? _____

Which operation will you do next? _____

Write your answer here: _____

We completed this assignment together.

_____   _____
(Parent's signature)   (Child's signature)

Dear Families,

While most of our students have mastered simple addition and subtraction, they may continue to make errors in certain kinds of problems, such as adding money and interpreting word problems. These are two major pitfalls and this activity should help students avoid both.

For this homework, please help your child to keep all of the decimals in a straight line. This is critical when adding money— and the main thing they forget to do when adding together amounts like two dollars, $4.52, and 83 cents. Without lining up the number correctly, they will end up with an unreasonable answer. Encourage your child to make exaggerated decimal points on each money problem. Point out that remembering to always line up the cents in the ones place should also keep everything else lined up properly.

When students have difficulty with word problems, they often have not read them very carefully, and therefore miss some of the information. Many test writers also mix the information in word problems, giving some of the information in numerical digits and the rest in words. These problems should help your child in both areas at once.

Sample Problem

Susan had $4.78. She found four pennies on the sidewalk. Then her mom gave her a weekly allowance of five dollars. How much money does Susan have now?

$ •   (money Susan had)

$ •   (pennies Susan found)

+ $ •   (Susan's allowance)

$ •   (total money Susan has now)

Let's work on this together.

Directions: Read and work the following addition and subtraction problems. Be sure to show your work. Hint: When you work with money problems, remember to keep the decimal points lined up.

1. Zana, Kathryn, Emily, and Becky are going to the mall with Becky's mother. Each of the girls has some money to spend. Zana has twelve dollars and fifty-two cents, Kathryn has $16.50, and Emily has $6.78. Becky is taking only a quarter because her mother is going to give her money at the mall. How much money together are the girls taking to the mall? _____

2. Jeff and Chris saved money to go to the baseball game. They needed $25.00 to get into the game and buy hot dogs and drinks. They had already saved $17.65. How much more money did they need? _____

3. Maelee and her mother are at the grocery store to buy some steaks for $6.85, some fresh corn for ninety-five cents, a quart of strawberries for $1.29, and five cans of soda totalling two dollars and fifty cents. How much money do they need to pay the cashier before they leave? _____

4. Students at Oak Hill School are selling bags of popcorn to raise money for a field trip. Mrs. Smith's class has sold $258.00 worth of popcorn. Mrs. Child's class has sold three hundred eighty-five dollars worth of popcorn and Mrs. Blake's class has sold seventy-four dollars and fifty cents worth of popcorn. How much have all three classes sold together? _____

We completed this assignment together.

_____   _____
(Parent's signature)   (Child's signature)

Dear Families,

It is important for children to understand one of the most basic concepts in the study of fractions: equivalent fractional amounts. Without understanding this concept, your child may have difficulty moving beyond addition and subtraction of fractions that have like denominators.

This homework asks your child to represent fractions by shading parts of a rectangle. The goal is for your child to describe how the fractions are equivalent based on what she or he notices about the shaded rectangles.

Your child will also need to create some visual representations of fractions. Please help your child to make the divisions in the rectangles relatively accurate. That will help her or him better see the equivalence. Also, reinforce fraction concepts by using the terms "numerator" and "denominator" where appropriate. The denominator is the numeral written under the fraction bar and tells the number of parts a whole is divided into. The numerator is the numeral written above the bar. It tells the number of parts of the whole that are being counted.

Sample Problem

We did this in class.

Look at the fractions below and notice that each denominator is the numeral 6. These rectangles have been divided into six equal parts. Look again at the fractions and notice the numerator. Shade each rectangle to represent the fraction.

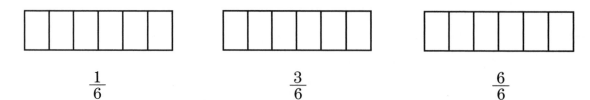

$$\frac{1}{6} \qquad\qquad \frac{3}{6} \qquad\qquad \frac{6}{6}$$

Which fraction represents the smallest amount? _____

Which fraction represents the largest amount? _____

Which fraction represents half? _____

Let's work on this together.

Directions: Look at the fractions below and shade each rectangle to represent the fractions. Then answer the questions.

$$\frac{1}{2} \qquad \frac{2}{4} \qquad \frac{4}{8} \qquad \frac{8}{16}$$

What do you notice when you look at the space that is shaded? What do you think is true about all of the answers above?

Divide and shade the rectangles below to represent each set of equivalent fractions.

Set 1

$$\frac{1}{4}$$

$$\frac{2}{8}$$

Set 2

$$\frac{1}{3}$$

$$\frac{2}{6}$$

We completed this assignment together.

_____
(Parent's signature)

_____
(Child's signature)

Geometry

Many people think only of computation when they think of math, but more and more state assessments are testing children's mathematical abilities far beyond basic computation. For example, in geometry students are expected to know the difference between plane and solid figures, how to find the area and perimeter of regular and irregular spaces, and the meanings of terms such as "vertices" and "faces." Even if these topics are not included in your district curriculum, you never know what might pop up on a norm-referenced test. It is important to expose students to these concepts in order to begin building a solid foundation so that students will be ready for the next steps in geometry.

Page 50 ● Skill: Terms for Three-Dimensional Shapes

It is important to work with three-dimensional shapes as a class before using this activity as homework. Be sure to cover a variety of solid shapes such as a cube, square pyramid, prism, cone, and cylinder. If possible, have students work with a flat version of each shape that they can cut out and assemble into an actual three-dimensional representation.

Be sure each child has completed the sample problem on the parent page before you send the paper home.

In the sample problem, students will be able to visually compare a flat and three-dimensional version of the same figure. Help students label the parts of a square pyramid.

In the homework activity, students will review the terms used with three-dimensional shapes. They will also be able to cut apart and assemble a cube. **Note:** Photocopy this homework on two separate sheets of paper so children can cut out the pattern.

Answers to Sample Problem: vertices, faces, edges.

Page 52 ● Skill: Comparing Three-Dimensional Shapes

If possible, have students create three-dimensional representations of these shapes from patterns to take home for use with the homework. However, if students have already had exposure to this content, they should be able to complete the homework with just the illustrations.

Answers to Sample Problem: 6 faces, 12 edges, 8 vertices, die or "number cube."

Page 54 ● Skill: Symmetry

The concept of symmetry can be fun to demonstrate. Try giving students a variety of experiences to find lines of symmetry. You can start by using chalk to lightly draw lines on objects in the classroom. Challenge students to determine if you made two equal sides. (Use chalk because it can easily be wiped off of most objects.)

You can also demonstrate symmetry by providing students with a variety of shapes and asking them to fold the shapes in various ways to see if they can get both sides to be the same. If the resulting two sides are congruent, or the same, they have found a line of symmetry. Students also enjoy drawing the missing half of objects. Rather than create all of these pictures yourself, invite students to fold a piece of paper in half and draw only one half of an object. Then pass the paper to a classmate to complete the missing parts on the other side of the line of symmetry. Be sure to use the correct terms in this activity: symmetry, symmetric, symmetrical, asymmetry, asymmetric, and asymmetrical.

Answers to Sample Problem: Students should draw in the other half of the circles.

Page 56 ● Skill: Proper Names for Geometric Shapes

For many students, geometry is the one area of math in which they can excel. They love making the three-dimensional figures, learning the different kinds of angles, working with a protractor, and seeing how shapes fit together. You can make geometry more fun by spreading the lessons throughout the year and by taking time to make all of those objects in the class. Along the way, be sure your students are learning the correct names for both plane and solid figures. This activity is intended as a review of common geometric terms.

Answers to Sample Problems: 1. ray 2. intersecting lines 3. point 4. line segment 5. perpendicular lines 6. parallel lines.

Page 58 ● Skill: Measuring Angles

In previous lessons we discussed using the proper terminology in geometry. With this lesson, be sure your students can give a logical explanation for why it is called a "tri-angle," and that they already know the names of angles (obtuse, acute, right) before you send the homework home. **Note:** This activity requires that students have access to a protractor.

You may also want to introduce terms such as "hypotenuse," "equilateral triangle," and "scalene triangle" to students. They usually enjoy knowing big and unusual words and can have fun showing off a little at home.

Answers to Sample Problem: angle A = 80 degrees, angle B = 35 degrees, angle C = 65 degrees; acute.

Dear Families,

Your child needs to know the names of solid, three-dimensional figures and be familiar with their correct terminology. This lesson is designed to review these terms.

In the square pyramid below, there is a square bottom with four triangles attached at each side of the square. The triangles meet at a point at the top. Each of these flat areas (triangles and the square) is called a face. Each of the places where two faces touch is called an edge. The square pyramid has four edges around the bottom and four edges where the triangles meet for a total of eight. Where the edges come together to form a corner or point is called a vertex. If you have more than one vertex, they are called vertices. The square pyramid has five vertices.

Sample Problem

We did this in class.

Label the parts of these square pyramids. The one on the left appears as a flat figure and the one on the right appears as a three-dimensional figure.

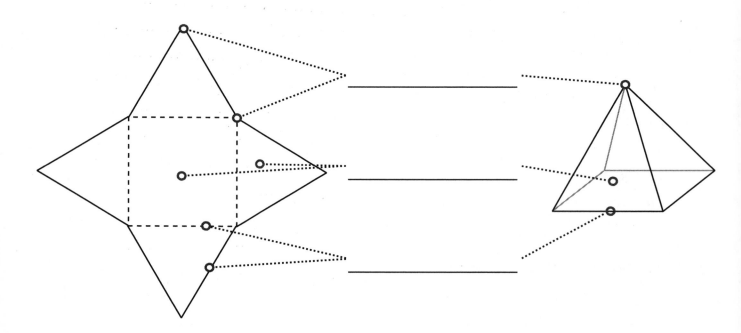

Let's work on this together.

Directions: Follow the step-by-step directions to use the pattern on this page to create a cube. Then answer the questions. Remember to return the cube to school.

• Using a colored pencil or pen, trace over the solid lines of the cube pattern.

• Lightly shade each face.

• Color in a dot at the end of each line.

• Cut out the pattern along the solid lines.

• Fold in at each dotted line. Where each edge meets, affix a piece of tape to hold the cube together.

1. How many edges are on your cube? _____

2. How many vertices are on your cube? _____

3. How many faces are on your cube? _____

We completed this assignment together.

_____
(Parent's signature)

_____
(Child's signature)

Dear Families,

Your children have learned about solid figures and the correct terms used to describe them. This homework will help students compare the various figures and find examples of each one around your home.

Use the paper models that we have constructed in class and/or the illustrated models, to help your child review the proper names for each solid figure. Then help count the correct number of faces, edges, and vertices on each and record the information on the chart. (Remember that the faces are the flat parts of the shape; the edges are where two faces meet; the vertices are where edges meet to make a corner or point.)

Finally, go on a scavenger hunt to find examples of each three dimensional shape in your home. If you are having trouble, try going outside to look. Think very big and very small!

Sample Problem

We did this in class.

Shape	Faces	Edges	Vertices	Example
Cube				

Let's work on this together.

Directions: Across the top of this chart you will see the correct names for parts of solid figures: faces, edges, and vertices (the plural form of vertex). Along the side are the names of familiar solid figures: cube, rectangular prism, cone, cylinder, and triangular prism.

Look at the illustrated models of these shapes. Then complete the chart telling the correct number of faces, edges, and vertices for each figure. We have provided some answers for you.

Shape	Faces	Edges	Vertices	Example
Cube	6	12	8	
Rectangular Prism				
Cone		1		
Cylinder	3			
Triangular Prism	5			

We completed this assignment together.

_____   _____
(Parent's signature)   (Child's signature)

Dear Families,

To learn about symmetry, students must first recognize that drawing a line of symmetry on a figure or an object divides it into two identical halves. Some objects have no line of symmetry; some have only one; some have several. This homework includes examples of all three.

The final activity asks your child to draw the missing part of a symmetrical figure. If your child has difficulty with this, try folding the paper in half on the dotted line. Then put the paper against a window and have the child trace the part he can see. When the paper is unfolded, he will have created the missing part.

Sample Problem

We did this in class.

The dotted line is a line of symmetry for each figure. Draw the part that should be on the other side of each line. It should mirror the part you can see.

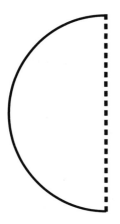

Directions: Follow the directions in each section to complete the activities.

Draw a line of symmetry (a line that will divide the figure into two identical pieces) on each of these objects.

Let's work on this together.

A B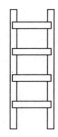

Some objects have one line of symmetry. Some objects are asymmetrical (which means they do not have a line of symmetry). Others have many ways to draw lines of symmetry. On each of these objects, draw as many lines of symmetry as you can.

  G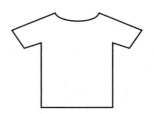

Draw the missing half of each object on the other side of the line of symmetry.

We completed this assignment together.

_____   _____
(Parent's signature)   (Child's signature)

Dear Families,

More and more state assessments are testing children's mathematical abilities far beyond basic computation. For example, students are expected to be able to identify shapes using the correct terminology. You can help your child get ready for the next steps in geometry by encouraging her or him to identify these shapes with real-life examples as you come across them. For example, at a traffic intersection, point out that the streets are like intersecting lines. Ask your child to identify the shape of traffic signs such as one indicating "stop" (octagon) or "yield" (triangle). In the grocery store, your child can identify the general shape of an orange (sphere) or soda can (cylinder). This homework activity is a review of geometric terms.

Sample Problems

We did this in class.

Match the geometric shape in the left column with the correct term in the right column. Hint: There is one term listed whose shape is not shown.

1. ⟶ line

2.  point

3. • line segment

4. •———• perpendicular lines

parallel lines

5.  ray

6. 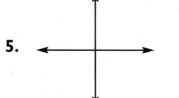 intersecting lines

Let's work on this together:

Directions: Match the geometric shape in the left column with the correct term in the right column. Hint: There is one term listed whose shape is not shown.

1. 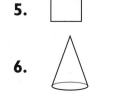   cube

2. ▭   circle

3. ◯   octagon

4. ▱   rectangle

5. ▢   pentagon

6. ⬭ (cone shape)   pyramid

7. (pyramid shape)   cylinder

8. ⬡ (hexagon)   triangle

9. (sphere)   cone

10. (octagon)   sphere

11. (cylinder)   quadrilateral

12. (cube)   hexagon

                                                           square

We completed this assignment together.

_____   _____
(Parent's signature)   (Child's signature)

Dear Families,

The students in our class have been learning to use a protractor to measure angles. You may not have used one of these tools for many years, so here is a refresher on how they work.

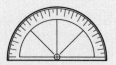

There are 360 degrees in a circle. A protractor is shaped like half of a circle, so the numbers around the outside edges go from 1 to 180. (They also go from 180 to 360, but we're not using that part for now.) To measure an angle, we are trying to determine how far apart the two intersecting lines are. We measure these in degrees. Simply lay the protractor down so that the hole in the center is exactly at the point where the two lines meet and the zero is on the horizontal, or bottom line. Now look to see where the second line of the angle is. Read the number that is there, and that is the number of degrees of the angle.

You and your child will be measuring three types of angles. Those that are exactly 90 degrees are called square angles, right angles, or 90 degree angles. Those with fewer than 90 degrees are called acute angles and those with more than 90 degrees are called obtuse angles.

Note: This activity requires students to use a protractor.

Sample Problem

We did this in class.

How many degrees are in each angle of this triangle?

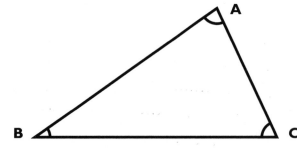

Angle A = _____

Angle B = _____

Angle C = _____

Is the shape a right triangle, an acute triangle, or an obtuse triangle?

_____

Let's work on this together.

Directions: Letters A, B, and C have been used to label the angles on these triangles. Use your protractor to measure the angles in each of the triangles below. Then write the number of degrees in each angle and the word *right*, *equilateral*, *acute*, or *obtuse*. What do you notice about the triangles when you add the number of degrees in each of the three angles?

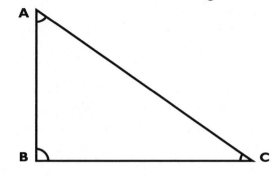

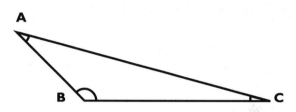

_____ + _____ + _____ = _____
  A   B   C

_____

_____ + _____ + _____ = _____
  A   B   C

_____

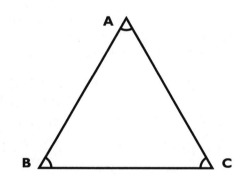

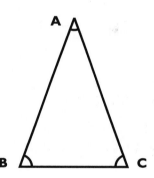

_____ + _____ + _____ = _____
  A   B   C

_____

_____ + _____ + _____ = _____
  A   B   C

_____

We completed this assignment together.

_____
(Parent's signature)

_____
(Child's signature)

Measurement

Often, the lowest scores on state and national assessments in math are in measurement. This concept has always been a challenge for students, especially in working with both standard and metric units. While students will need to be able to work within each system, and should know the tools, units, and appropriate situations for using which type of measurement, they may not be asked to do any converting from one system to the other.

The lessons in this section cover a few of the many kinds of measurement that your students may encounter on a state or national assessment. Be sure you have given your students adequate exposure to and experience with reading a thermometer to measure temperature, using volume measures such as gallons and liters, using rulers and meter sticks for linear measurement, and using a balance scale for mass.

> ### Page 63 ● Skill: Using the Correct Measurement Tool

If possible, provide your students with experiences using a variety of authentic measuring devices. Allow students to use a graduated cylinder to measure water or sand, a ruler that measures both centimeters and inches, and a balance scale using grams, ounces, and nonstandard units of measure such as a paper clip.

> Be sure each child has completed the sample problem on the parent page before you send the paper home.

Answers to Sample Problems: ruler; answers will vary; yardstick; answers will vary.

> ### Page 65 ● Skill: Measuring Time: Calendar

Prepare students for this homework by copying a page from your school calendar or a blank calendar. Make a copy for each child. Allow them to use colorful markers and different symbols or marks to indicate important things in that month, such as the date a fund-raiser will begin, the date report cards go home, the days when there is no school, holidays, birthdays of classmates, and so on. Be sure you spend some time clarifying that the previous month ended on the day before this month began and the next month will start one day after this month ends.

Teach your students the traditional mnemonic poem: Thirty days hath September, April, June, and November. All the rest have thirty-one, except for February alone.

Answers to Sample Problems: Sunday; Tuesday; Wednesday.

Page 67 ● Skill: Calculating Area & Perimeter

This homework should be sent home only after you have explicitly taught "area." These lessons are much easier if you begin by using a grid (see the inside back cover for a reproducible grid with 1-centimeter squares). This will help students to see that area is just another way of saying "how many squares are there?" Later you can use plain paper and students will still retain a visual idea of area.

Students have a very difficult time understanding the concept of "square" measurement and they rarely use that descriptor when describing area. But area is measured in "square units" of inches, feet, yards, miles, centimeters, or kilometers. This activity is a great way to introduce students to area measurement because it actually uses squares to find the area of their foot, making it fun and keeping the use of squares firmly in their minds the first time they encounter this type of measurement.

You probably want to follow this up with several activities in which students count square units to determine area of regular and irregular shapes.

Answer to Sample Problem: Answers will vary.

Page 69 ● Skill: Comparing Area & Perimeter, Part I

This activity (along with the grid found on the inside back cover) introduces students to area and perimeter. Use the homework page as a follow-up or as a review page long after students understand the concepts.

The assignment asks students to make a comparison between area and perimeter. This activity is the opposite of Comparing Area & Perimeter, Part 2. In Part 1, each of the shapes has the same area, but the perimeter is drastically different because of the shape of the figures. To introduce this concept to students, try using another number with several factors, such as 24. (Shapes will be 1 x 24; 2 x 12; 3 x 8; 4 x 6.) Work through the whole process, just as the children will be doing for homework. For maximum concept development, do not tell the students how to do this; let them work through it themselves. Then be sure they see the relationship of using 1, then 2, then 3, then 4 for one side of the figure, and be sure they realize that these are multiplication facts. This is an excellent way to teach how to find the area of a square or rectangle, especially if students discover it themselves.

Answers to Sample Problem: A = 36; P = 24.

Page 71 ● Skill: Comparing Area & Perimeter, Part 2

This activity is the opposite of Comparing Area & Perimeter, Part 1. It was created to help students see that the perimeter of an object can remain the same, even if the area is different. You may choose to do these two activities back to back or you may spread them out and use one of them as a review of skills previously learned. Either way, this is a valuable experience for students.

Answers to Sample Problem: P = 24; A = 32.

Page 73 ● Skill: Drawing Figures to Scale

Students may have a difficult time understanding "scale drawings," unless you help them with some real-life situations. If you are lucky enough to have a tile floor in your classroom, try having your students create a drawing of the classroom by duplicating on paper each tile on the floor. It won't take them long to realize that they could not possibly create a drawing the same size as the real floor—and they will have a great introduction to scale drawings. If your floor does not have square tiles, gather as many rulers as possible and have the students line them up, end to end across the room. After students count the rulers (or tiles), have them make scale drawings, allowing 1 centimeter for each ruler (or tile), to determine the size of the room "to scale." (At this stage of their development, it is probably better to have them actually use as many rulers as they need to cross the room instead of putting down a ruler and moving it. At the introductory stages of this concept, they need to see that each ruler will equal 1 inch on their drawing. Hint: To make this easier, use the 1-centimeter grid provided on page 97 so students can simply count the squares instead of having to measure them. You can also extend this activity by creating a scale drawing of your hallway or the cafeteria.

Answers to Sample Problem: 2 inch x 3 inch rectangle.

Dear Families,

You may not be aware that on nationwide tests students perform the least well on measurement. "Measurement" on tests has three parts: Students must know which tool is used to get which kind of information (for example, a ruler is used to measure length; a clock is used to measure time), which tool to use in a particular situation (for example, you would not use a stopwatch to measure the hours in a day; you would not use a cup to measure the amount of water in a pool), and what measurement term goes with which tool (a ruler measures in inches or centimeters; a scale measures in ounces and pounds or grams and kilograms). Students must also know which standard units of measurement correspond with which metric ones. (Meters are similar to yards on a yardstick; grams are similar to ounces.) Students do not usually need to know how to convert between standard and metric units.

You can best assist your child by using the correct measurement terms in your daily conversation and by allowing her or him to use the most basic measurement tools. Allow your child to use a ruler to measure the length of a shoe, help you use the scales in a store to get the weight of fruit, and use a cup measure to add the correct volume of milk to a recipe.

Sample Problems

We did this in class.

Write the name of the tool you would use to measure these objects. Then measure and record each length. Remember to include the unit of measurement on that tool.

To measure the length of your hand, use a _____ (tool).

My hand is _____ (number) _____ (units) long.

To measure the length of our classroom, we use a _____ (tool).

Our room is _____ (number) _____ (units) long.

Skill: Using the Correct Measurement Tool

Let's work on this together.

Directions: Here is a list of things that we measure. Complete the chart by writing the name of the tool we can use to measure things and the unit of measurement that the tool gives us. A few are done for you.

How to Measure Weight	
Tool	
Standard units	ton
Metric units	

How to Measure Linear Distance (Height, Length, Width)	
Standard tool	
Metric tool	
Standard units	feet
Metric units	meter

How to Measure Volume	
Tool	measuring spoon, measuring cup
Standard units	tablespoon, cup
Metric units	milliliter

How to Measure Time	
Tool	stopwatch, timer, watch, sundial, calendar
Standard & metric units	minutes, years

How to Measure Temperature	
Tool	
Standard units	Fahrenheit degrees
Metric units	Centigrade degrees

Word Bank

miles
meterstick
day
hour
teaspoon
kilogram
pint
yardstick
inch
liter
scale
quart
gram
gallon
ounce
pound
centimeter
second
yard
kilometer
ruler
thermometer

We completed this assignment together.

_____
(Parent's signature)

_____
(Child's signature)

Dear Families,

When we think of measuring time, we usually think about clocks or stopwatches. One area of time measurement we tend to overlook is using a calendar. While your child probably has been doing calendar activities almost every day since kindergarten, there are a couple of things that even intermediate elementary students typically do not understand about calendars.

The main concept students miss is that, simply put, we don't skip any days. We never say, "There won't be a Tuesday this week." But when students look at a month that ends on a Monday, they often have trouble recognizing that the next month will begin on a Tuesday. Help your child to see that the months of a calendar can go together just like a puzzle. The first day of one month just starts where the last day of the previous month ended. This simple concept will help them to correctly answer several of the questions on this homework.

Another concept that students fail to understand is that when we talk about "weeks" we can move vertically on a calendar. Thus, if we are talking about March 17 being on a Friday, then "one week later" will also be on a Friday. Two weeks later will likewise fall on a Friday. This will still be true even if we move to the next month. Four weeks after March 17 will still be a Friday, but it will be April 14.

Sample Problems

We did this in class.

On what day of the week does this month begin?

_____

On what day does it end?

_____

On what day of the week does November begin?

_____

OCTOBER 2006						
S	M	T	W	T	F	S
1	2	3	4	5	6	7
8	9	10	11	12	13	14
15	16	17	18	19	20	21
22	23	24	25	26	27	28
29	30	31				

Let's work on this together.

Directions: Use the calendar below to answer these questions. Be sure to write the dates correctly: no abbreviations, write out the month, then the number of the day, followed by the year. (Example: March 17, 2006.)

JANUARY 2006
S M T W T F S
1 2 3 4 5 6 7
8 9 10 11 12 13 14
15 16 17 18 19 20 21
22 23 24 25 26 27 28
29 30 31

FEBRUARY 2006
S M T W T F S
1 2 3 4
5 6 7 8 9 10 11
12 13 14 15 16 17 18
19 20 21 22 23 24 25
26 27 28

MARCH 2006
S M T W T F S
1 2 3 4
5 6 7 8 9 10 11
12 13 14 15 16 17 18
19 20 21 22 23 24 25
26 27 28 29 30 31

APRIL 2006
S M T W T F S
1
2 3 4 5 6 7 8
9 10 11 12 13 14 15
16 17 18 19 20 21 22
23 24 25 26 27 28 29
30

MAY 2006
S M T W T F S
1 2 3 4 5 6
7 8 9 10 11 12 13
14 15 16 17 18 19 20
21 22 23 24 25 26 27
28 29 30 31

JUNE 2006
S M T W T F S
1 2 3
4 5 6 7 8 9 10
11 12 13 14 15 16 17
18 19 20 21 22 23 24
25 26 27 28 29 30

JULY 2006
S M T W T F S
1
2 3 4 5 6 7 8
9 10 11 12 13 14 15
16 17 18 19 20 21 22
23 24 25 26 27 28 29
30 31

AUGUST 2006
S M T W T F S
1 2 3 4 5
6 7 8 9 10 11 12
13 14 15 16 17 18 19
20 21 22 23 24 25 26
27 28 29 30 31

SEPTEMBER 2006
S M T W T F S
1 2
3 4 5 6 7 8 9
10 11 12 13 14 15 16
17 18 19 20 21 22 23
24 25 26 27 28 29 30

OCTOBER 2006
S M T W T F S
1 2 3 4 5 6 7
8 9 10 11 12 13 14
15 16 17 18 19 20 21
22 23 24 25 26 27 28
29 30 31

NOVEMBER 2006
S M T W T F S
1 2 3 4
5 6 7 8 9 10 11
12 13 14 15 16 17 18
19 20 21 22 23 24 25
26 27 28 29 30

DECEMBER 2006
S M T W T F S
1 2
3 4 5 6 7 8 9
10 11 12 13 14 15 16
17 18 19 20 21 22 23
24 25 26 27 28 29 30
31

1. On what day of the week is the first day in July? _____

2. What date is exactly two weeks after the first day in July? _____
What day of the week is this?

_____

3. What date is exactly two weeks before the first day in July? _____
What day of the week is this?

_____

4. How many Mondays are in March? _____
What other months have the same number

of Mondays? _____

_____

5. List the months with only 30 days.

_____

_____

6. What day of the week is the last day in January? _____ What day of the week is the first day in February? _____ What day of the week is the last day in February? _____ What day of the week is the first day of March? _____

We completed this assignment together.

_____
(Parent's signature)

_____
(Child's signature)

Dear Families,

When someone mentions finding the area of a figure, we usually think of the familiar formula: multiply length times width (l x w = area). That works if we are trying to find the area of a square or rectangle. It is not much help if the figure is an unusual shape. This homework involves finding the area covered by your child's bare foot.

Here are some suggestions to make this project easier:

- When only part or half of a square is covered, try to find another part of a square that you can visually add to it to make a complete square and count it as one.

- Have the child stand on the paper as you trace around her or his foot. Try to hold the pencil straight up and down so that you don't go in too far on the arch of the foot. Do not go between the toes.

- Counting the squares will be easier if you put a check or X in each box. You can also use different colored pens or pencils, changing colors after every ten boxes. Then you can count by tens to add up the total number of checks.

Sample Problem

We did this in class.

Put your thumb on the grid (at right). Trace around it. Now count the number of complete squares that were covered by your thumb. Now look at the squares that were only partly covered. Find two that can be added together to count as one square. Continue that process until you have counted all of the squares. How many squares did your thumb cover? _____

My Thumb

Skill: **Calculating Area & Perimeter**

Let's work on this together.

Directions: Put one foot on the grid that is attached to this page. Ask an adult to trace around your foot. Then let the adult help you find the area in square centimeters that is covered by your foot. Count carefully. If there is a box that is only partway inside of the line of your foot, try to find another partial box that you can add to it to make one whole box and count that as one. Record the square units covered by your foot and return both pages to your teacher.

The area of my foot is _____ square centimeters.

Bonus:

Trace another object using the grid at right. Try to find the area in square centimeters.

The area of _____

is _____ square

centimeters.

We completed this assignment together.

_____   _____

(Parent's signature)   (Child's signature)

Dear Families,

This homework assignment asks you and your child to compare area and perimeter. Help your child make five figures, one square and four rectangles, each with an area of 36 squares. (Remember the area is the amount of space inside a figure.)

This page is designed to provide your child with a review of many concepts. Help your child with the project, but try to have her or him see how to do it independently. Eventually she or he should see that each figure is actually a factor of 36 (6 x 6 makes the square) and in so doing should realize that this is the "formula" for finding the area of a rectangle or square: length times width (l x w).

Part 1 of this project is for your child to see how the perimeter of a shape might change, even though the area may remain constant. Be sure to take a good look at the completed chart and make those kinds of comparisons with your child.

Sample Problem

We did this in class.

On this grid, make a square that is 6 squares long and 6 squares wide.

What is the area of this square?

_____

What is the perimeter of this square?

_____

Let's work on this together.

Directions: Attached to this page you will find a sheet of graph paper on which you will draw one square and four rectangles that each have an area of 36 squares. Label each figure A, B, C, D, and E. Next, color each figure a different color. Then, complete the chart below.

Area is the space inside the figure.
Perimeter is the distance around the outside of a figure.

	Color	Length	Width	Area	Perimeter
A					
B					
C					
D					
E					

I. Which of the five shapes (A, B, C, D, or E) had the smallest perimeter? _____

2. Which of the five shapes had the greatest perimeter? _____

We completed this assignment together.

_____   _____
(Parent's signature)   (Child's signature)

Dear Families,

This homework assignment asks you and your child to compare area and perimeter. Help your child make six figures—one square and five rectangles each with a perimeter of 24 squares. (Remember the perimeter is the distance around the outside of a figure.)

This page is designed to provide your child with a review of many concepts. Help your child with the project, but try to have her or him see how to do it independently.

Part 2 of this project is for your child to see that the area of a shape might change, even though the perimeter may remain constant. Be sure to take a good look at the completed chart and make those kinds of comparisons with your child.

Sample Problem

We did this in class.

On this grid, make a rectangle that is 8 squares long and 4 squares wide.

What is the perimeter of this square?

_____

What is the area of this square?

_____

Let's work on this together.

Directions: Attached to this page you will find a sheet of graph paper on which you will draw one square and five rectangles that have a perimeter of 24 squares. Label each figure A, B, C, D, E, and F. Next, color each figure a different color. Then, complete the chart below.

> Perimeter is the distance around the outside of a figure. Area is the space inside the figure.

	Color	Length	Width	Perimeter	Area
A					
B					
C					
D					
E					
F					

1. Which of the six shapes (A, B, C, D, E, or F) had the smallest area?_____

2. Which of the six shapes had the greatest area?_____

We completed this assignment together.

_____
(Parent's signature)

_____
(Child's signature)

Dear Families,

Drawing figures to scale is a new concept for most elementary students, so this activity is designed to introduce them to this concept at its most basic level. Be sure your child knows why we draw things to scale—because we cannot always draw the pictures of objects in their actual size. Children may not realize that they have been drawing to scale since they first held a crayon and drew a house—one that fit on the page and only represented a real building.

On the student page there are four instances in which your child is asked to create a scale drawing. The figures will be 1, 2, or 3 inches across, but they are intended to represent much larger figures. The questions about perimeter refer to the numbers that are on the figure—not the actual inches that the child just drew—and the perimeter of the figure of the fictional character.

Sample Problem

We did this in class.

Let's make a scale drawing of this sheet of paper. This paper is $8\frac{1}{2}$ inches wide by $11\frac{1}{2}$ inches long. To make this easy, let's round off the numbers to 8 x 12. Now let 1 inch on your ruler equal 4 inches on the sheet of paper.

How wide should the rectangle be?

_____

How long should it be?

_____

Draw a scale drawing of this sheet of paper here:

Let's work on this together.

Directions: Each of the four problems below requires you to use a ruler and create a scale drawing. A "scale" drawing is a representation of a larger object. Ask an adult to help you to draw the figures correctly and answer the question about each one.

1. Tom drew a shape that was 5 inches long on each side. The box was a square. Use a ruler and make a square like Tom's. Have 1 inch in your drawing equal to 5 inches of Tom's drawing.

Now write the number 5 on each of the sides. What is the perimeter of Tom's shape? P = _____ inches.

Draw what you think Tom's shape looked like.

2. Kevin drew a shape that was a rectangle. Two sides were 10 inches long; two sides were 5 inches long. Use a ruler. Let 1 inch on the ruler be equal to 5 inches of Kevin's shape.

Now write the correct numbers on the sides of the shape. What is the perimeter of Kevin's shape?

P = _____ inches.

Draw a rectangle like Kevin's.

3. Cathy drew a shape that was an equilateral triangle. Each side was 5 inches long. Use your ruler and make 1 inch equal to 5 inches of Cathy's triangle.

Now write the correct numeral on each side.

What is the perimeter of Cathy's shape? P = _____ inches.

Draw what Cathy's shape looked like.

We completed this assignment together.

_____
(Parent's signature)

_____
(Child's signature)

Logical Thinking

Children do not instinctively think logically. This is a skill that must be taught and practiced so that it eventually comes naturally and easily. One way to teach logical thinking is to have students think in an "if . . . then" pattern. This means that if one thing is true, then another, logical consequence must also be true. One simple example of this kind of reasoning follows: If the number is greater than 9 then it must have at least two digits.

Another way to think logically is to learn the answer to a problem by figuring out what the answer cannot be. If the answer is not above 50 and it is not an odd number and it is not more than one digit and it is not larger than 3, it must be 2. If you have eliminated all of the other possibilities, the one that remains must be the answer.

The activities in this section are designed to foster logical thinking in students.

Page 77 ● Skill: In/Out Box, Part 1

Present these first as whole-group problems. Then as small-group problems, ask students to work in groups of two or three to make up their own stumpers for the other groups to solve. When you are fully confident that students understand the In/Out Box concept, prepare some of these for individual work. About a week or so later, send this home as a review lesson. Remember that most of your parents will be unfamiliar with this concept, so be sure your students know it well enough to explain it to them.

> Be sure each child has completed the sample problem on the parent page before you send the paper home.

Answers to Sample Problem: add 4; 2 becomes a 6.

Page 79 ● Skill: In/Out Box, Part 2

How many times have you had students work word problems and end up with totally unreasonable answers? Do they subtract when they should multiply? Add when they should subtract? This lesson is intended to help that situation.

One valuable lesson you can teach students is there are two operations (addition and multiplication) that, when performed on a numeral, will result in creating a larger numeral, and two operations (subtraction and division) will result in a numeral with a smaller value. You may even want to create a reminder chart of this in your classroom. Then, when your students are working word problems, teach them to ask themselves, "Should the answer to the question be a larger number or a smaller number than the one I began with?" (If Susie goes to the store with $5.00 and spends $2.48, will she have more or less money when she comes home?") Once they are thinking in this logical way, students should realize whether their answer is or is not in line with the thinking they have done even before they began their calculations.

Possible Answers to Sample Problem: multiply by 3; A = 9; B = 45.

Page 81 • Skill: Mystery Number, Part 1

Here are two sets of Mystery Number clues that you can use in class before you send home the assignment. **Note:** Both in class and for homework, students will need a copy of a 100 Chart. Try writing one clue at a time on the board or chart paper.

Discuss what the clues and the terminology mean and help students fold and/or mark their papers after each clue so that they see how they are eliminating possibilities. The comments following the clues are to help the students in their logical thinking. Help your students to realize they can often figure out what an answer is by figuring out what it isn't!

Sample 1: The number is on the bottom half of the 100 Chart, so I _____. (Child folds the top half back.) The number is odd, so I _____. (Child replies that they marked out all of the numbers that ended with 2, 4, 6, 8, or 0.) The two digits add up to 14, so it could be _____. (Child realizes that there is more than one possibility and still needs another clue.) The second digit is larger than the first, so the mystery number is _____. (In this case the number is 59.)

Sample 2: The number is on the top half of the 100 Chart, so I _____. (Child folds the bottom half back.) The number is even, so I _____. (Child marks out all of the numbers that end with 1, 3, 5, 7, or 9.) The two digits add up to 7, so it could be _____. (Child realizes that there is more than one possibility and still needs another clue.) The second digit is 5 larger than the first, so the mystery number is _____. (In this case the number is 16.)

Answer to Sample Problem: The mystery number is 12.

Page 83 • Skill: Mystery Number, Part 2

Be sure you do several Mystery Number activities with your students in the classroom. Explain the logic of finding out what the number can't be as a way of determining what it actually is.

Laminate several 100 Charts, or lay clear acetate transparency sheets over the charts and allow students to complete practice papers using dry-erase markers. Each time they can mark their chart to indicate what has been eliminated from the 100 possible numbers on the chart. Then they can simply wipe their page clean with a damp paper towel and they are ready for the next problem.

Another way to do these is to have students use copies of a 100 Chart and fold it each time so that they gradually decrease the number of numerals that are left to choose from. For example, if the clue says that the Mystery Number is on the top half of the 100 Chart, they would fold back the second half, thus eliminating those numbers and allowing them to concentrate on only half as many possibilities.

Be patient if students don't get it the first couple of times you do these. It takes time and practice to think logically.

Answer to Sample Problem: The mystery number is 13.

Dear Families,

The In/Out Box is a device that is commonly found on tests in mathematics, but it is something with which many parents are not familiar. This homework activity is intended to provide additional practice on something that your child has experienced in the math classroom, but probably has not seen anywhere else.

Treat the In/Out Box as if it were a machine that makes changes to a numeral. Your child must try to figure out what *has* happened to a numeral that has gone into the box and/or what *will* happen to a numeral that goes into the box. For example, if a 3 goes into the box and an 8 comes out, we can determine that the box adds a 5 to whatever goes into it. Once your child has determined the relationship between the number going in and the number coming out, she or he has solved the mystery.

Sample Problem

We did this in class.

In	Out
1	5
3	7
5	9
2	?

What happens in the box? _____

What would come out if you put in a 2? _____

Directions: Below are several In/Out Boxes. Try to figure out what happens in the box and write that action above it. The first one is done for you.

Let's work on this together.

Box 1:
add 5

In	Out
3	8
12	17
34	39

Box 2:

In	Out
3	15
6	30
10	50

Box 3:

In	Out
12	2
54	44
89	79

Box 4:

In	Out
15	6
30	21
32	23

Box 5:

In	Out
2	12
5	30
7	42

Box 6:

In	Out
16	8
24	12
48	24

Box 7:

In	Out
8	4
15	11
35	31
84	80

Box 8:

In	Out
10	22
36	48
41	53
73	85

Box 9:

In	Out
3	6
6	12
7	14
15	30

We completed this assignment together.

_____

(Parent's signature)

_____

(Child's signature)

Dear Families,

With this In/Out Box activity, your child needs to do two steps: First she or he will determine what is happening in the box. Second, your child will have to actually do some of the calculating and determine what numerals have been "fed" into the box.

The important step here is getting children to recognize the relationship between the numerals that are given. If your child is still having difficulty seeing these relationships, first ask your child if the numeral coming out of the box is of greater or lesser value than the one that went into the box. Help your child to see that two operations (addition and multiplication) will produce an answer that is larger than what they began with and that two operations (subtraction and division) will produce an answer that is smaller than the one with which they began. This simple realization can help your child with many future math problems!

Once your child can see that the "out" numeral is larger or smaller than the one going in, all they need to do is determine which operation was done to create that new numeral. This may or may not be obvious when you look at the first time the numbers went in and came out. (For example, if 3 goes in and 6 comes out, the operation may be multiplication by 2 or it may be adding by 3.) In these cases, you will need to look at all three relationships to determine what all three have in common.

Sample Problem

We did this in class.

What happens inside the box?

_____

_____

What would go in space A?

_____

What would go in space B?

_____

In	Out
4	12
5	15
A	27
15	B

Let's work on this together.

Directions: For boxes 1–3, you must determine what happens in the box and then write in the correct response for what is coming out of the box. For boxes 4–9, you must determine what is happening in the box and what numeral was put into the box. The first one is done for you.

Box 1:
subtract 1

In	Out
98	97
75	74
12	11
9	8

Box 2:

In	Out
8	64
5	40
9	72
10	?

Box 3:

In	Out
15	3
20	4
45	9
30	?

Box 4:

In	Out
16	21
68	73
100	105
?	49

Box 5:

In	Out
7	28
10	40
6	24
?	36

Box 6:

In	Out
49	7
63	9
14	2
?	5

Box 7:

In	Out
59	48
73	62
92	81
?	5

Box 8:

In	Out
80	8
20	2
50	5
?	7

Box 9:

In	Out
43	64
21	42
67	88
?	36

We completed this assignment together.

_____

(Parent's signature)

_____

(Child's signature)

Dear Families,

This homework assignment is designed to foster your child's logical thinking. We have completed Mystery Number puzzles in our classroom, but in order for this to be successful as a homework assignment, there are some terms you will need to know. Please be sure your child knows these terms, too. It will make the puzzles easier to solve.

✓ **Digit:** A digit is simply a numeral. The number 23 has two digits.

✓ **Even:** An even number is one that ends with a 0, 2, 4, 6, or 8.

✓ **Odd:** An odd number is one that ends with a 1, 3, 5, 7, or 9.

✓ **Top and bottom of the 100 Chart:** Look at the 100 Chart. All of the numbers on the top half of the chart are less than 50; all those on the bottom half are more than 50.

✓ **Ones place:** The number on the right side of a two-digit numeral. In the number 23, the 3 is in the ones place.

✓ **Tens place:** The number on the left side of a two-digit numeral. In the number 23, the 2 is in the tens place.

✓ **Right side of the 100 Chart:** Numbers on the right side of the 100 Chart have numerals greater than 5 in the ones place.

✓ **Left side of the 100 Chart:** Numbers on the left side of the 100 Chart have numerals less than 5 in the ones place.

Note: This homework should include a copy of a 100 Chart.

Sample Problem

We did this in class.

The mystery number is an even number. (Cross out all of the odd numbers.) The mystery number is less than 22. (Cross out all of the even numbers larger than 22.) The mystery number has two digits. (Cross out all of the numbers with one digit.) The two digits in the mystery number add to 3. The mystery number is _____.

Use this chart to find the Mystery Number:

1	2	3	4
11	12	13	14
21	22	23	24
31	32	33	34

Let's work on this together.

Directions: Use the clues below to help you figure out the mystery numbers. Each time you read a clue, cross out or eliminate some numbers from the 100 Chart. After the last clue, when you think you have the mystery number, go back and reread each clue to be sure you correct.

Mystery Number #1 Clues:

The number is on the left side of the 100 Chart. (Fold your chart in half.)

The two digits add up to 6. (Circle the numbers that it could be.)

The number is odd. (Cross out all of the even numbers.)

The first digit is larger than the second digit.

The mystery number is _____.

Mystery Number #2 Clues:

The number is on the right side of the 100 Chart. (Fold your chart in half.)

The number is even. (Cross out the odd numbers.)

The two digits add up to 13. (Circle the numbers that add up to 13.)

The second digit is 1 smaller than the first.

The mystery number is _____.

Mystery Number #3 Clues:

The number is on the bottom half of the 100 Chart.

The number is odd.

The two digits add up to 9.

The first digit is 7 larger than the second.

The mystery number is _____.

Mystery Number #4 Clues:

The number is on the top half of the 100 Chart.

The number is odd.

The number has only one digit.

The number is less than 3.

The mystery number is _____.

Mystery Number #5 Clues:

The number is on the bottom half of the 100 Chart.

The two digits add up to 14.

The mystery number is odd.

The second digit is larger than the first.

The mystery number is _____.

Mystery Number #6 Clues:

The number is on the bottom half of the 100 Chart.

The number is odd.

The two digits add up to 11.

The first digit is 5 larger than the second digit.

The mystery number is _____.

We completed this assignment together.

_____
(Parent's signature)

_____
(Child's signature)

Dear Families,

Most students do not naturally think logically about number problems. These Mystery Number puzzles are designed to foster logical thinking by having students analyze clues to an unknown numeral. Each new clue narrows the possible choices for the number, until soon there is only one logical choice left that will satisfy all of the clues and answer the question.

Your child may think you are working backwards, because instead of figuring out directly what the mystery number is, each clue will, instead, help her or him figure out what it isn't, until eventually there is only one choice left. To make this easier, use the 100 Chart in one of two or three ways. You may choose to help your child fold it each time so that only part of the chart is visible. On other occasions, you may allow your child to use certain colors of crayons or markers to indicate what numbers have been eliminated from the possible choices. Let your child make an X, a circle, a line through, or trace around the box each time in a different color.

These Mystery Numbers involve the use of the 100 Chart. Sometimes this type of activity requires using a T chart. The goal of each of these activities is the same: improving logical thinking and number sense.

Note: This homework should include a copy of a 100 Chart.

Sample Problem

We did this in class.

Use this chart to find the Mystery Number:

The mystery number is an odd number.
(Cross out all of the numbers that are even.)
The mystery number is less than 21.
(Cross out all of the odd numbers larger than 21.)
The mystery number has two digits.
(Cross off the one-digit odd numbers.)
The two digits in the mystery number add up to 4.
The mystery number is _____ .

1	2	3	4
12	12	13	14
21	22	23	24
31	32	33	34

Directions: Use the following clues to find out the mystery number! Remember to fold your 100 Chart or mark it in some way so you will know how each clue has helped you get closer to solving the mystery.

Mystery Number #1 Clues:

The number is on the top half of the 100 Chart.

The two digits add up to 7.

The number is even.

The second digit is 5 larger than the first digit.

The mystery number is _____.

Mystery Number #2 Clues:

The number is on the top half of the 100 Chart.

The two digits add up to 11.

The number is even.

The second digit is larger than the first.

The mystery number is _____.

Mystery Number #3 Clues:

The number is on the bottom half of the 100 Chart.

The two digits add up to 17.

The number is odd.

The second digit is larger than the first.

The mystery number is _____.

Mystery Number #4 Clues:

The number is on the top half of the 100 Chart.

The two digits add up to 5.

The number is even.

The first digit is 1 larger than the second.

The mystery number is _____.

Mystery Number #5 Clues:

The number is on the right side of the 100 Chart.

The two digits add up to 10.

The second digit is 2 larger than the first digit.

The mystery number is _____.

Mystery Number #6 Clues:

The number is on the right side of the 100 Chart.

The number is even.

The mystery number is a double number.

The number does not include an 8.

The mystery number is _____.

We completed this assignment together.

_____
(Parent's signature)

_____
(Child's signature)

Graphing

Students need to know three things about graphs. First, they need to know how to interpret the information they see on a graph. They need to get beyond "which one has the most" and "which one has the least" and make real judgments about the data. They also need to understand the scale used on a graph and how pictographs are used to display information. Finally, they need to know how to create a graph. Students should know the parts of a graph, why they are there, and how to use them. The bar graph is the graph most often found on tests. That is what is emphasized in this section. Be sure to expose your students to circle graphs (pie charts) and line graphs as well.

Page 87 ● Skill: Interpreting a Graph

> Be sure each child has completed the sample problem on the parent page before you send the paper home.

Your own class can create a graph just like the one on page 88. It is a good idea to do this before you send it out as homework. Simply list the colors of backpacks on the chalkboard or chart paper and have students sign their name beside the color that best describes their pack. (Some students' packs will have many colors, so they must make an observation of which color is the dominant one.) Then transfer that information to a class graph that you create as a whole group. Remember to create the graph and properly label the axes, do not allow the bars to touch, and give the graph a title.

Then have students practice coming up with some truth statements about their own graph. After the easiest and most obvious ones have been voiced, make a couple of deeper observations yourself to get your students started on the track to writing their own detailed truth statements.

Answers to Sample Problem: Answers will vary.

Page 89 ● Skill: Creating a Bar Graph

Because this assignment asks students to correctly create a bar graph, it should not be sent home unless you have already taught students how to do this. And the best way to teach it is to actually do it. Try having your own class make a chart of their favorite flavors of ice cream. (Limit the choices to no more than six unless you have a very large group with which to work.) Then you should construct a class graph while each child in the room makes one to match yours. This modeling is something that is often overlooked in math classes. If you walk students through the process step by step and discuss each one, they will understand the process much better. They can compare their completed graphs to yours for accuracy. After they have done the whole-group activity and the homework assignment, try giving them a new set of data to graph.

Answers to Sample Problem: (clockwise from top) vertical axis, title, data, scale, horizontal axis.

On many state assessments students are asked to create a chart or a graph from data—much like this assignment—so it becomes even more vital that we present this information to students. Remember that you will need to present this several times before you can assume that students can remember to do all of these steps independently.

Answers to Sample Problem: The parts of the graph should have the correct labels.

Page 91 ● Skill: Pictographs

Your students need to know about the scale of a graph and why pictographs are sometimes chosen over numerical graphs. To guide students to understand the importance of using a proper scale (not always one space on a graph to represent one object) try creating a graph of something for which you know there will not be enough spaces on the chart paper. You may want to chart the numbers of interlocking cubes in the classroom. While a standard box of cubes should contain about 1000—100 each of 10 colors—there are not enough spaces on a typical sheet of graph paper to create a regular bar graph. After you list the colors and start coloring in the spaces, and students realize that you cannot fit the information on the space, start asking for suggestions. Some students may suggest that you simply add on more paper to make the graph larger. You can try this, but soon, even the chart paper will become unwieldy. Eventually you want to lead the discussion to realize that you could count by 5s, 10s, 25s, and so on.

This is a perfect time to introduce pictographs. They serve the same purpose as altering the scale of the graph: Each picture represents multiple objects. They also allow the reader to see the information at a glance and to make observations quickly. Try making your graph two ways—once by altering the counting and once by adding pictures.

Answers to Sample Problems: 1. 55 2. 125 3. Week 4 4. 50 5. 240 candy bars in total.

Page 93 ● Skill: Mean, Median, Mode, Range

If you saved the charts from other graphs made this year, pull them out now. Use the data on those charts to teach your students these four ways of interpreting information on a graph. Remind them that they may be asked to find the mean, median, mode, or range from just a set of numbers, not necessarily from a graph.

This is another activity that will require a lot of modeling and practice. Students often remember what to do to find these things, but they mix up which method goes with which term. As with most of these activities, teach each one of these concepts several times before assuming that students can do it independently.

Answers to Sample Problem: Mode = 12; Median = 27; Mean = 31.4; Range = 62.

Dear Families,

A graph is simply a picture of mathematical information. We use graphs to see the data clearly, making it easier to compare and interpret. In this homework, your child will write "truth statements," requiring her or him to look at the graph and decide what the graph is showing. Your child will probably begin with the simplest of observations, such as "There were more black backpacks than any other color. There were fewer yellow backpacks than any other color." These are acceptable statements, however, as your child has more practice in looking at mathematical information, encourage her or him to create more detailed observations such as "The number of red plus the number of purple backpacks equals the number of green backpacks."

Encourage your child not to write opinions such as "No one liked yellow backpacks." We do not really know this from the information on the graph. We can say there were no yellow packs, but we do not know for sure why this is true. There could be many reasons that no yellow backpacks were in the classroom.

Sample Problem

We did this in class.

This graph shows how some students get home from school. Write three things you can learn from looking at this graph.

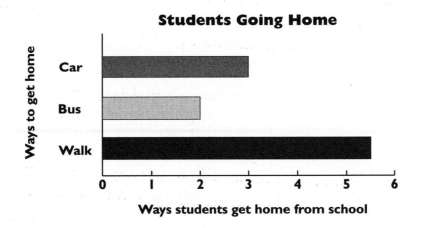

Observations: _____

_____

_____

Skill: Interpreting a Graph

Let's work on this together.

Directions: Study this graph that tells the colors of backpacks and the numbers of each color of backpack in one classroom. Then write five truth statements—five things you can learn from looking at the graph.

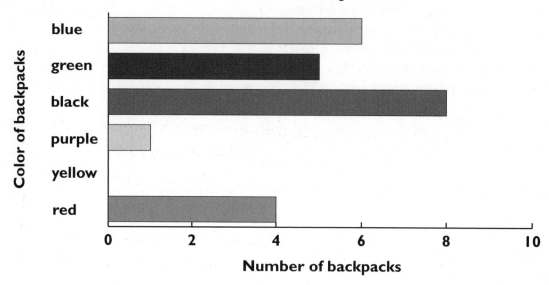

Kids' Backpacks

Truth Statements

1. _____

2. _____

3. _____

4. _____

5. _____

We completed this assignment together.

_____ _____
(Parent's signature)   (Child's signature)

Week-by-Week Homework for Building Math Skills • Scholastic Teaching Resources

Dear Families,

Our class has been studying graphing and we have been making our own graphs. Now students are ready to do one independently. There are several elements that must be included in a bar graph: a title for the graph, labels for the horizontal and vertical axes, information such as numbers and words, and the proper placement of data. All of these elements are necessary in order for a graph to be complete.

Many state mathematics assessments are including activities like this one, where students need to transfer the data to a bar graph. It is important that your child remember to include every element and to do this process correctly.

Sample Problem

We did this in class.

Label the parts of this graph: title, vertical axis, horizontal axis, scale, data.

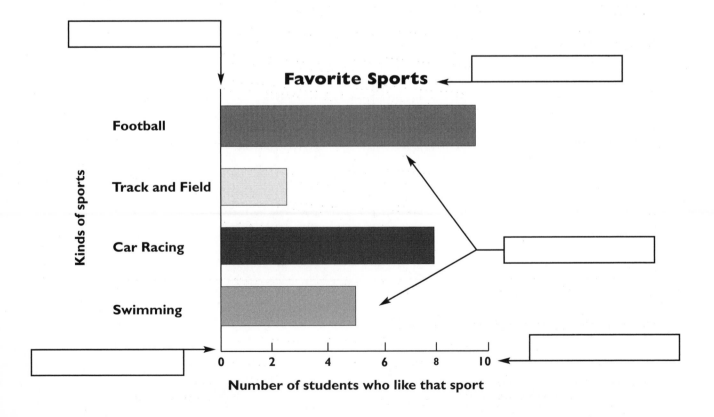

Let's work on this together.

Directions: Place the data below on a bar graph. Write the flavors of ice cream up the vertical axis and numbers across the bottom. (Don't forget the zero!) Give a label to each axis. Then draw bars on the graph to represent the data. Finally, give your graph a title.

chocolate chip	│ │ │ │ │ │ │ │ │ │
vanilla	│ │ │ │ │
strawberry	│ │ │ │ │ │
rocky road	│ │ │ │
bubble gum	│

We completed this assignment together.

_____
(Parent's signature)

_____
(Child's signature)

Dear Families,

In our study of graphs we have learned about circle graphs (pie charts), line graphs, and bar graphs. Now it is time to look at a new kind of bar graph: the pictograph. In this kind of graph, a small picture is used to represent the data. Partial pictures are used if the numbers are between the amounts represented by the pictures. These are sometimes confusing for students. Be sure your child knows to look for the "key" much as she or he would on a map. The key tells you what each picture on the pictograph represents.

Sample Problems

We did this in class.

Answer the following questions about this pictograph about Mrs. Fisher's class' chocolate sales.

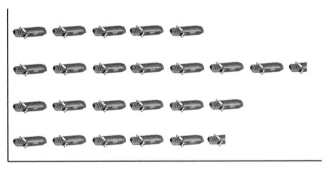

Mrs. Fisher's Chocolate Sales

Key

= 10 candy bars

1. How many candy bars did Mrs. Fisher's class sell the first week of the chocolate sales? _____

2. How many candy bars did Mrs. Fisher's class sell the last two weeks of the chocolate sales? _____

3. In which week did Mrs. Fisher's class sell the fewest candy bars? _____

4. How many did they sell that week? _____

5. How many candy bars in total did Mrs. Fisher's class sell in four weeks? _____

Let's work on this together.

Directions: Middleport Elementary School sold T-shirts as a fundraiser. This graph called a "pictograph" shows the number of shirts each grade level sold. Look at the key. If each T-shirt represents 10 shirts, what do you think half of a T-shirt represents? Look carefully at the pictograph and answer the questions.

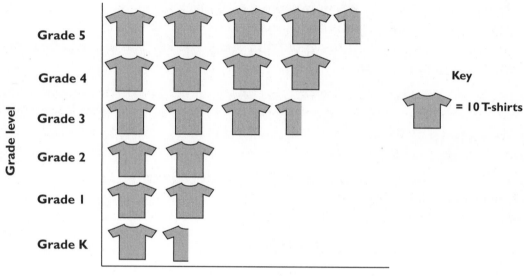

Middleport Elementary T-shirt Sales

Key = 10 T-shirts

1. Which grade level sold the most shirts? _____

2. Which grade level sold the fewest shirts? _____

3. Which two grades sold an equal number of shirts? _____

4. How many shirts were sold in grades 1 and 2 combined? _____

5. How many shirts were sold in grade 5? _____

6. How many more shirts did the fifth graders sell than the fourth graders? _____

7. How many more shirts did the fifth graders sell than the kindergartners? _____

8. What was the total number of shirts sold at Middleport Elementary School? _____

We completed this assignment together.

_____   _____
(Parent's signature)   (Child's signature)

Dear Families,

There is more to making observations from a graph than just writing truth stateme[...]
tonight's homework we will review other ways of interpreting data on a graph. Here[...]
quick refresher on these methods.

✓ **Mean:** The "average" is the same as the "mean." Add the total of all the numbers and divide by how many numbers you added.

✓ **Median:** The median number is simply the middle number. The easiest way for students to find this is for them to list all of the numbers in order from largest to smallest. Then they should cross off the largest and smallest numbers, moving toward the center until all of the numbers are crossed off but one. If you have an odd number of numerals, there will clearly be a median number. If you have an even number of numerals, you will end up with two "median numbers." To find the true median, you should find the amount halfway between the two.

✓ **Mode:** The mode is the number that appears most often in the data.

✓ **Range:** To determine the range, simply subtract the smallest number from the largest one.

Sample Problem

We did this in class.

Find the mean, median, mode, and range of this set of data:

$$12, 35, 74, 12, 48, 12, 27$$

Mode: Which number appears most often in this set of numbers? _____

Median: Arrange the numbers from largest to smallest. Include every number even if it is there more than once. Cross off the top and bottom numbers until you find the median. What is the median number? _____

Mean (Average): Add together all of these numbers. Then divide the total by 7. Why should you divide by 7? _____
What is the mean of these numbers? _____

Range: Write down the largest number in the group. Subtract the smallest number. This difference is called the range. What is the range of these numbers? _____

Directions: Look at the graph below. Answer the following questions. Be sure to show your work.

Fruit We Like

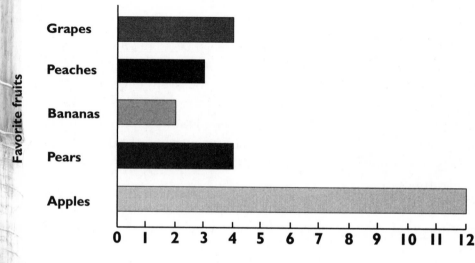

1. What is the mean number (average) of the data on this graph? _____

2. What is the mode of the data on this graph? _____

3. What is the range of the data on this graph? _____

4. What is the median number of the data on this graph? _____

We completed this assignment together.

_____   _____
(Parent's signature)   (Child's signature)

Answer Key

Page 13:
1. greatest value: 875; least value: 578 2. greatest value: 843; least value: 348 3. greatest value: 952; least value: 259 4. greatest value: 621; least value: 126 5. greatest value: 964; least value: 469 Bonus: The numbers are in reverse order when changing from greatest to least value.

Page 15:
1. 4, four ones 2. 40, four tens 3. 4000, four thousands 4. 400, four hundreds 5. 400, four hundreds 6. 40, four tens 7. 4, four ones 8. 4000, four thousands Bonus: The 4 would change if we added 10 to this number. The new number would be 5753. The 5, 7, and 3 stay the same. Answers will vary. 5843, 5443, 7743

Page 17:
1. (order will vary) 37 + 63, 93 + 7, 73 + 27, 55 + 45, 61 + 39, 87 + 13, 22 + 78, 41 + 59, 18 + 82, 67 + 33 2. 36, 48, 75, 29, 12 3. 36 + 64, 48 + 52, 75 + 25, 29 + 71, 12 + 88 4. Answers will vary.

Page 19:
Rings should be around these 23 combinations: 4 + 7 + 9; 8 + 12; 7 + 6 + 7; 9 + 11; 17 + 3; 7 + 13; 3 + 9 + 8; 6 + 3 + 11; 7 + 13; 6 + 14; 4 + 8 + 8; 4 + 4 + 12; 5 + 13 + 2; 10 + 10; 11 + 4 + 5; 12 + 8; 4 + 9 + 4 + 3; 8 + 3 + 6 + 3; 7 + 5 + 8; 5 + 8 + 3 + 4; 8 + 7 + 5; 9 + 4 + 3 + 4; 7 + 5 + 8 (Some may seem like the same problem, but the numbers have appeared in different order or in different places in the puzzle.)

Page 21:
1. 55, 44, 33, 22, 11 2. 10, 12, 14, 16, 18 3. 45, 54, 63, 72, 81 4. 48, 36, 24, 12, 0 5. 300, 350, 400, 450, 500 6. 6, 8, 7, 9, 8 7. 64, 128, 256, 512, 1024 8. 40, 30, 35, 25, 30 9. 16, 15, 20, 19, 24

Page 23:
Four dimes and one nickel; three dimes and three nickels; two dimes and five nickels; one dime and seven nickels; one quarter and two dimes; one quarter, one dime, and two nickels; one quarter and four nickels; nine nickels

Page 25:
1. 25 2. 13 3. 39 4. rectangle; triangle 5. 26 6. 2 7. 38 8. 11, 12, 10, 14; 47 9. 1, 2, 3, 4, 5, 6, 7, 8, 9; 45 10. 2

Page 27:
Part 1: A dot should be placed on 74, 75, 76, 77, 88, 98, 108, 117, 116, 115, 114, 103, 93, 83, 74. They should be connected to form a circle. **Part 2:** A dot should be placed on 48, 47, 46, 45, 44, 43, 33, 34, 24, 14, 15, 16, 17, 27, 37, 38, 48. They should be connected to form a hat. **Part 3:** A dot should be placed on 44, 54, 64, 74, 75, 76, 77, 67, 57, 47. They should be connected to form a square. The completed puzzle makes a snowman with a top hat.

Page 33:
1. 8 2. 12 3. 16 4. 18 5. 14 6. 22 7. 24 8. 20 9. 13 10. 21 11. 10 12. 130 13. 19 14. 15 15. 23 16. 50 17. 70 18. 110

Page 35:

	1	2	3	4	5	6	7	8	9	10
1	2	3	4	5	6	7	8	9	10	11
2	3	4	5	6	7	8	9	10	11	12
3	4	5	6	7	8	9	10	11	12	13
4	5	6	7	8	9	10	**11**	**12**	**13**	14
5	6	7	8	9	10	11	**12**	**13**	**14**	15
6	7	8	9	10	11	12	13	**14**	**15**	16
7	8	9	10	**11**	**12**	13	14	15	**16**	17
8	9	10	11	**12**	**13**	**14**	15	16	17	18
9	10	11	12	**13**	**14**	**15**	**16**	17	18	19
10	11	12	13	14	15	16	17	18	19	20

Page 37:

	1	2	3	4	5	6	7	8	9	10
1	1	2	3	4	5	6	7	8	9	10
2	2	4	6	8	10	12	14	16	18	20
3	3	6	9	12	15	18	21	24	27	30
4	4	8	12	16	20	24	28	32	36	40
5	5	10	15	20	25	30	35	40	45	50
6	6	12	18	24	30	**36**	**42**	**48**	54	60
7	7	14	21	28	35	**42**	**49**	**56**	63	70
8	8	16	24	32	40	**48**	**56**	**64**	72	80
9	9	18	27	36	45	54	63	72	81	90
10	10	20	30	40	50	60	70	80	90	100

Page 39:
Chart: 9, 18, 27, 36, 45, 54, 63, 72, 81, 90. 1. The numerals in the ones place decrease in value; the numerals in the tens place increase in value. 2. Each time you add the digits in the answer to a nines multiplication problem, the answer is always 9. 3. The answers are opposites as you go up and down the column: 45 is opposite of 54; 36 is opposite of 63; yes

Page 41:
1. clue: together, larger; 641 cards 2. clue: how much left, smaller; $8.25 3. clue: how many more, smaller; 35 jumps

Page 43:
1. clue: divided into groups of three, altogether, division, multiplication or addition, 42 2. clue: spent, and, who spent more, addition, subtraction, Ben, $ .23 3. clue: and, altogether, addition, multiplication or addition, 25

Page 45:
1. $36.05 2. $7.35 3. $11.59 4. $717.50

Page 47:
Half of each rectangle should be shaded. Students should notice that the same amount of the rectangle is shaded using different fractions. In Set 1 and Set 2, the fractions should be represented as accurately as possible.

Page 51: 1. 12 edges 2. 8 vertices 3. 6 faces

Page 53:
Cube: 6 faces, 12 edges, 8 vertices; Rectangular prism: 6 faces, 12 edges, 8 vertices; Cone: 2 faces, 1 edge, 1 vertex; Cylinder: 3 faces, 2 edges, 0 vertices; Triangular prism: 5 faces, 9 edges, 6 vertices; Answers for examples of each figure will vary.

Page 55:
Vertical: A, spoon, pineapple, T-shirt; Horizontal: B; Vertical and horizontal: X, oval, ladder; None: hand, G; other half of objects should be drawn in

Page 57:
1. pentagon 2. rectangle 3. circle 4. quadrilateral 5. square 6. cone 7. pyramid 8. hexagon 9. sphere 10. octagon 11. cylinder 12. cube

Page 59:
Right: A = 55 degrees, B = 90 degrees, C = 35 degrees; Obtuse: A = 30 degrees, B = 135 degrees, C = 15 degrees; Equilateral: A = 60 degrees, B = 60 degrees, C = 60 degrees; Acute: A = 40 degrees, B = 70 degrees, C = 70 degrees; In each triangle, the number of degrees should add to 180.

Page 64:
Scale; ounce, pound; gram, kilogram; ruler, yardstick; meterstick; inch, yard, mile; centimeter, kilometer; teaspoon, pint, quart, gallon; liter; second, hour, day; thermometer

Page 66:
1. Saturday 2. July 15; Saturday 3. June 17; Saturday 4. four; February, April, June, August, September, November, December 5. four; September, April, June, November 6. Tuesday; Wednesday; Tuesday; Wednesday

Page 68:
Answers will vary.

Page 70:
Five figures; one should be a 6 x 6 square. The others are all rectangles; colors to vary. Sizes include: 1 x 36, area 36, perimeter 74; 2 x 18, area 36, perimeter 40; 3 x 12, area 36, perimeter 30; 4 x 9, area 36, perimeter 26; 6 x 6, area 36, perimeter 24. Greatest perimeter, 1 x 36 rectangle = 74. Smallest perimeter, 6 x 6 rectangle = 24. Page 72: The square figure is 6 x 6, perimeter 24, area 36; rectangles are 7 x 5, perimeter 24, area 35; 8 x 4, perimeter 24, area 32; 9 x 3, perimeter 24, area 27; 10 x 2, perimeter 24, area 20, 11 x 1, perimeter 24, area 11. Greatest area, 6 x 6 square = 36. Smallest area, 11 x 1 rectangle = 11

Page 72:
The square figure is 6 x 6, perimeter 24, area 36; rectangles are 7 x 5, perimeter 24, area 35; 8 x 4, perimeter 24, area 35; 9 x 3, perimeter 24, area 27; 10 x 2, perimeter 24, area 20, 11 x 1, perimeter 24 feet, area 11

Page 74:
1. There should be a square, 1 inch on each side;

each side should be labeled with the numeral 5; P = 20 inches. 2. There should be a rectangle, 2 inches by 1 inch; the long sides should be labeled with a 10; the short sides with a 5; P = 30 inches 3. There should be a triangle with three equal sides each 1 inch long; each side should be labeled with a 5; P = 15

Page 78:
1. add 5 2. multiply by 5 3. subtract 10 4. subtract 9 5. multiply by 6 6. accept divides by 2 or half the original number 7. subtract 4 8. add 12 9. accept multiply by 2 or double the original number

Page 80:
1. subtract 1; 8 2. multiply by 8; 80 3. divide by 5; 6 4. add 5; 44 5. multiply by 4; 9 6. divide by 7; 35 7. subtract 11; 16 8. divide by 10; 70 9. add 21; 15

Page 82:
1. 51 2. 76 3. 81 4. 1 5. 59 6. 83

Page 84:
1. 16 2. 38 3. 89 4. 32 5. 46 6. 66

Page 88:
Answers will vary. Responses can be considered correct if they can be verified by the information on the graph. Students should not write that black is the favorite color. There may be more black packs, but that doesn't mean that the kids like it the most. We do not know if the backpacks were borrowed, were hand-me-downs, or were chosen by the parents.

Correct responses might include: There were zero yellow backpacks. There was 1 fewer red backpack than green. There were 2 more black backpacks than blue. Black and blue backpacks added together equals 14 backpacks.

Page 90:
Some answers will vary. Completed graph must include a title of the child's choice; vertical axis should be labeled something like "Favorite kinds of ice cream" and should have all five flavors of ice cream listed. Horizontal axis should have numbers to at least 10, followed by a label for the axis like "Numbers of kids." The data should extend to the right, across the graph, with one box colored in to represent each students' preference. The graph should be neat and the bars should not touch.

Page 92:
1. Grade 5 sold the most shirts. 2. Kindergarten sold the fewest shirts. 3. The first and second grades sold equal numbers of shirts. 4. Grades 1 and 2 combined to sell 40 shirts. 5. Grade 5 sold 45 shirts. 6. The fifth graders sold 5 more shirts than the fourth graders. 7. The fifth graders sold 30 more shirts than the kindergartners. 8. There were a total of 175 shirts sold in Middleport Elementary School.

Page 94:
1. Mean = 5 2. Mode = 4 3. Range = 10 4. Median = 4